GLÉNANS
WEATHER
FORECASTING

Beaufort Scale Force Six

GLÉNANS WEATHER FORECASTING

A Manual for Yachtsmen

*Illustrations of Beaufort Scale
Wind Forces by
Laurence Bagley*

DAVID & CHARLES
Newton Abbot   London

Glénans Weather Forecasting is an
extract from *The New Glénans Sailing Manual*
also published by David & Charles.

British Library Cataloguing in Publication Data
Centre nautique des Glénans
    Glénans weather forecasting.
    1. Weather forecasting   2. Yachts and yachting
    I. Title
    551.6'3'0247971   QC995

    ISBN 0–7153–7911–9

© Editions du Seuil 1976
Weather Around the British Isles and the North Sea
© David & Charles 1980

Translation © James MacGibbon 1978

Illustrations of Beaufort Scale
© Laurence Bagley and
IPC Magazines Ltd 1973 (courtesy *Yachting Monthly*)

Photoset and Printed in Great Britain
by Redwood Burn Ltd, Trowbridge & Esher
for David & Charles (Publishers) Limited
Brunel House   Newton Abbot   Devon

Contents

Introduction to the British Edition   6

1 Tomorrow's Weather   7

2 The Life of the Atmosphere   11
The air   16
The air masses   24
Clouds   31
Fogs   40
Classification of the air masses   40
Wind   43
General circulation   49
The wind and the sea   54

3 The Weather   62
Maritime weather   63
Types of weather   95
Weather around the British Isles and in the
North Sea   110
Mediterranean weather   129

4 The Weather to Come   169

**5 Sources of Information for Practical
Meteorology**   178
British reports   178
French reports   188

Bibliography   190
Index   191

Introduction to the British Edition

The New Glénans Sailing Manual was first published in English in 1978. Within eighteen months of publication it was in its third impression. It seems to have become generally accepted as a manual of unimpeachable authority. Its five parts cover virtually everything there is to be written on seamanship but it is felt that a small volume of handy size on meteorology for yachtsmen would fulfil a purpose. So, as was done in France, the meteorology section from the manual appears on its own with some practical additions on the BBC shipping forecasts and, most importantly, a new section on 'British' weather, specially written for this edition by Mr F. J. Burton, formerly Chief Meteorological Officer at the Plymouth Meteorological Office, RAF Mountbatten. He kindly checked the translation of the meteorological section in the original manual.

The section on Mediterranean weather may not seem immediately relevant to British sailors as so many (alas!) cannot spare the time to take their own boats to that region. Nevertheless, it is right to retain it in this British edition for there is much general information to be learned from the behaviour of the atmosphere in a sea area that is so different from the Atlantic.

The Director of the French National Meteorological Service wrote that this short book succeeds in its aim of promoting greater safety at sea. Weather is, after all, the greatest hazard.

1 Tomorrow's Weather

At sea, tomorrow's weather is a matter of the utmost importance for us; unfortunately we are quite incapable of predicting it ourselves. Not so long ago, speculation still went on about the colour of the sky, the behaviour of the cat or the captain's rheumatism, and the predictions drawn from them were not necessarily wrong. We may not know how to do that any more, but thanks to the meteorological services, we now have access to information about the weather that old sailors could never have dreamed of imagining. It is entirely due to these services that nowadays we can have a pretty clear view of what lies ahead.

Meteorology has for long been denied due recognition. The meteorologists have a difficult role to play. They are working on complicated and problematical information, the evidence of which can be interpreted in more than one way by each forecaster. They work on a scale that is far beyond the needs of most of us, and this often leads to bitter disappointment and gives the impression that forecasting is a guessing game. The truth is that the real users of meteorological information – notably sailors and airmen who have very precise reasons to be interested in the forecasts – know that the reports are very reliable. The use of radar and satellites for exploring the sky, computers for sifting and assessing the information received, as well as the radical advance in the methods of deduction, all contribute to the increasing accuracy of forecasts.

If weather forecasts are still somewhat suspect, it is probably because there is a tendency to look on them as if they

Beaufort Scale Force Two-Three

were consumer products to be swallowed whole. It has to be realised first of all that a minimum of knowledge is needed for a full understanding of forecasts. Next, that they cover very wide areas and cannot take into account the variations in weather at any one particular point. Some of the work therefore remains to be done by the yachtsman himself. For amateur sailors, as for everyone else, a correct forecast of the weather is subject to two conditions: a correct interpretation of the bulletins; and an ability to deduce from them, with the help of one's own observations, the shape the weather will take in the locality where one is sailing.

To get a clear picture of the situation broadcast, it is not enough to know vaguely what is meant by the words *depression, anticyclone* or *cold front*. We might as well admit it: we can understand nothing of meteorology without taking the trouble to read up the subject and acquire more than a superficial knowledge of the principal atmospheric phenomena, their causes and what the overall pattern suggests. There is no doubt that this has to be done, and that is why we have included a whole chapter to study the subject in general: a rather dry chapter that is nothing else than an account of our research and that is somewhat outside the mainstream of this book. Boats are scarcely mentioned, and we even take off up into the mountains, where it might well be said we have no business. But the mountains are the very place to study pragmatically the behaviour of the air, before tackling the great spaces themselves, the clouds, the masses of air, the invisible slopes that exist in the sky and along which the wind flows. At this point we can already see the specialists raising their eyebrows: is this going to be a superficial re-hash of the subject? We are open to the charge; but an attempt to treat such a vast subject in a few pages is a calculated gamble and when forced to choose between clarity and exactness (although it is reprehensible to separate these two qualities) we have opted for clarity. We confess we feel passionately on the subject. That is not an excuse, but may go some way to explain why we have not always confined ourselves to professional terms.

The second chapter tries to summarise what is needed for the second part of the study – forecasting on a local scale, starting from personal observation, which can be useful only if one knows exactly the characteristics of the weather in the area as a whole, the *types of weather* that are most common there and the special characteristics likely to be met. We shall attempt therefore to define, at least in broad terms, *oceanic* weather and Mediterranean weather, two very different types, which we hope will have some practical bearing on conditions in many parts of the world. We conclude with a few considerations about forecasting itself.

centre of the earth

The radius of the Earth and the thickness of the troposphere are reproduced here on the same scale. All clouds are in the troposphere. Its thickness varies with its latitude

6 400 km

North Pole   7 km

11 km

earth

17 km

12 km

tropopause

troposphere

South Pole

2 The Life of the Atmosphere

Meteorology is an esteemed science, mainly because it tries to answer honestly the questions of persistent children. The sun warms the Earth – as everyone knows. But why does the air grow colder and colder with increase in altitude, although the sun is getting nearer and nearer? Why is it hot at the equator and cold at the poles? Why does that cloud stay still on the top of the mountain, although the wind is so violent? And why are there clouds? And wind? Where do they come from and where are they going?

We wave goodbye to the experts and those blessed with good memories, who can smile at such questions. Let us proceed gradually, step by step.

The sun radiates energy towards the Earth, a sphere surrounded by atmosphere. Part of this energy is reflected back towards space as the solar beams approach our planet, and has no effect on it. Another, quite small, part is absorbed by the atmosphere itself, which is slightly warmed by it (a light ray absorbed by an obstacle is in fact changed into heat). Another part is finally absorbed by the Earth's surface and warms it considerably.

Let it be appreciated from the start that, if the transfer of energy went in one way only, the temperature of the Earth would go on increasing and we would not be here to speak about it. But the Earth, like any heated body, radiates in its turn. Globally – that is the word – it radiates as much energy as it receives and a balance is established.

The first important point to be made is that in any one period of time, the ground absorbs about three times more

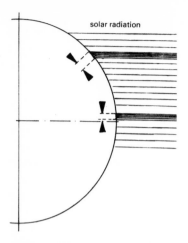

solar radiation

Solar radiation is uniform but in high latitudes it is spread over a greater surface than at the Equator

energy than the atmosphere above it. The ground is therefore, on average, hotter than the atmosphere and begins to heat it from below. This heating process is felt to a height of about 12km. From the Earth's surface up to 12km, the temperature therefore decreases with the altitude. This is the principal characteristic of this low stratum of the atmosphere, called the troposphere: the changing sphere. The thickness of this layer varies, according to the latitude (12km is only an average: it is much thicker at the equator than the poles); it varies too from one day to the next, and in the process creates the weather. Its upper limit is called the *tropopause*. Above that, and up to 50km, is the *stratosphere*, where the temperature increases slightly with height and in the lower part can be very turbulent. The higher regions are outside our scope.

Compared with the 6,400km radius of the terrestrial globe, the troposphere, with its altitude of 12km, may be relatively as thin as tissue paper around an orange; but this skin nevertheless contains 80 per cent of the total mass of air, and 90 per cent of the atmosphere's moisture; it is the core of what concerns us here – where all the clouds appear, and the majority of the phenomena that affect us.

The next question is: why is it cold at the poles and hot at the equator?

The sun's rays are parallel (or for our purposes can be considered to be), but the Earth is a sphere. The polar regions consequently get less heat because they receive less insulation per unit area of surface than the equatorial regions, which are far more exposed.

This simple answer is apparently satisfying, but it is in fact misleading, leading as it does to another difficult question. The calculation of the quantities of energy absorbed respectively by the equator and the poles reveals an enormous imbalance between the two regions that should result in a far greater difference of temperature than is in fact the case. It would appear that the equatorial regions should be terribly hot and the polar regions terribly cold, both of them equally uninhabitable. As this is not so, and if the temperature is, give or take a few pullovers, bearable almost everywhere, the reason is, obviously, that an atmospheric change occurs between the equator and the poles. This raises a new question: how does this change come about? The answer, this time, is more complicated and is the real purpose of meteorology.

Physics tells us that any body heated at a particular spot tends to spread out the heat through its entire mass. This dispersal is carried out through *conduction*, that is to say by contact, little by little, to the interior of the mass itself. But this does not happen on the planet Earth, for the ground is a bad conductor of heat. The process can also be effected through *radiation*. But the radiation of the Earth is almost entirely lost in space. Only a small part is reflected back by the clouds (which explains why the nights are not so cold when the sky is clouded over as when it is clear), but that is far from being sufficient to establish an equilibrium between the equator and the poles, for great quantities of heat have to be transferred.

Conduction and radiation are the only means of exchange

on the Moon, for instance. And temperatures of 200°C are registered there in sunny areas, and −100°C in areas in shade.

But the Earth has its atmosphere and oceans. Air and water are in themselves bad conductors of heat, but they can move. The air can also carry water, abstracted by evaporation from the wet parts of the planet. Can these two mobile elements, which seem to be constantly mixing, not contribute to equalising temperatures on the surface of the globe? And could this equalisation of temperatures not be, precisely, the reason why they move? This is really what the meteorologists have made clear: on the planet Earth, thermal exchanges happen essentially through the movement of huge fluid masses, some towards the poles, others from the poles towards the equator. The exchanges occur by *convection*.

There are also warm ocean currents, such as the Gulf Stream, that carry the heat of the tropical seas towards the north, and cold ocean currents, such as the Labrador Cur-

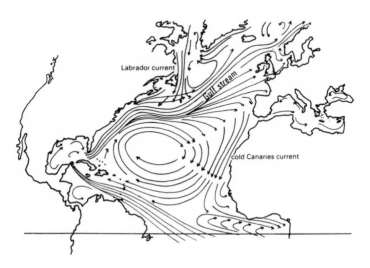

Principal currents in the North Atlantic

rent, flowing down in the opposite direction. These currents, however, move very slowly and account for only a small part of the exchange. Most is done by the atmosphere: the masses of warm equatorial air tend to move towards the poles and the masses of cold polar air to drift towards the equator.

As a result of this scheme of things, it might seem that, from now on, an explanation of the winds should be easy. One is entitled to expect the principal winds in the atmosphere to be north and south winds. But, if the standard patterns of the winds on the globe's surface, as they have been recorded by observations carried out over many years, are considered, one must think again. Those from the north and south don't figure in them (on balance, they cancel each other out); the normal winds are east and west: east winds in the equatorial and polar regions, west winds in the temperate regions. Apparently, again, the winds are, on average, very weak: hardly four miles per hour, but we know some blow far more strongly.

Here the children's questions begin to be provoking. One might answer them peremptorily and briefly thus: 'The Earth rotates on itself. As it is full of bumps and hollows, this rotary movement creates eddies in the air. Some of them turn in one direction, some in another; some point upwards,

Average winds at ground level

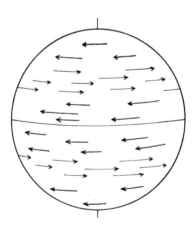

some down. Again, the oceans and continents heat up and cool down at different rhythms: their disparity of temperature creates other eddies, which appear and disappear periodically. The masses of warm air and the masses of cold air which try to ensure the exchanges between the equator and the poles are dragged into all these movements and thereafter go in unexpected directions. Moreover, when a mass of warm air and a mass of cold air meet, they absolutely refuse to mix: they clash with each other, and that in turn creates still more eddies, in which the wind is strong, and which move between the original great eddies. It's a little like a complex of cogwheels.'

No one need know more than this. But if you want to get to the heart of the matter, summon up all your patience, get right down to it, put on a thinking cap and examine the subject from the very beginning. Learn first of all what this air is, that we are speaking about (and which we breathe as well); next define precisely what we mean by an air mass, how it travels and what happens to it. We must in our minds glide along in the moving world of air. Only then will we begin to have some understanding of the amazing forces that quicken it.

The air

Air is composed of a mixture of gases, mainly oxygen and nitrogen. It contains as well a great quantity of water. This water can itself be in the gaseous form of water vapour, which is invisible; or else in liquid and visible form as clouds.

A point to be stressed is that the air contains a lot of water. Solar radiation, by heating the oceans and other moist parts of the Earth, causes great quantities of water to evaporate. It has been estimated that the sun, on good days, sucks up an amount equal to one glass full of water per hour per square metre of ocean. There are therefore thousands of millions of tons of water suspended in the air.

Air already weighs something. The ground therefore is

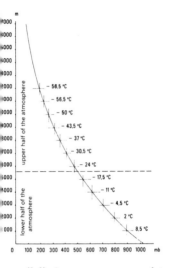
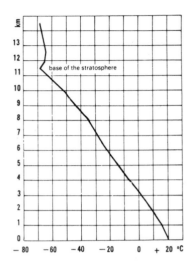

(*left*) Average pressure and temperature in relation to altitude;
(*right*) example of vertical distribution of temperature in the latitude of France

under pressure from the atmosphere. The *atmospheric press-ure*, at a given point on the surface of the globe, is equal to the weight of the column of air which rises above the spot. The pressure diminishes, naturally enough, with the altitude, but more gradually as it rises: the air is, in fact, compressible, and this compression is noticeable in its lower layers. Pressure and height are, in any case, closely related, and height is calculated by measuring pressure. The altimeters used in aircraft are in fact aneroid barometers. Yachtsmen also use aneroid barometers. In meteorology the unit of pressure used is the *millibar* (mb) with the average pressure at 0 altitude, or sea level, a trifle over 1,000mb.

The air, as we know, has a certain temperature, and in the troposphere this diminishes with altitude. The *vertical thermal lapse rate* or environmental lapse rate, which is the rate at which temperature decreases between the Earth's

17

surface and the tropopause, is on average 6°C per kilometre.

In short, any motionless parcel of air at a given point in the troposphere is defined by the three coordinates: temperature, pressure and humidity.

But a parcel of air is rarely motionless; and its characteristics are modified as soon as it moves. Moving air (the subject of our study) thus undergoes changes which can be justifiably referred to as different 'states'. It is important to analyse these states closely; that is the key to all that follows.

States of the air

Let us take the example of a wind arriving at the foot of a mountain, and compelled to rise to get over it. This is a somewhat special case in that the movement of the air is imposed here by the surface (*orographic* movement), while the movements in a free atmosphere have other origins. But it is illuminating.

We shall cross the mountain four times, with four different states of air.

First case

The air that arrives at the foot of the mountain contains water solely in the form of water vapour and in very small quantity (diagram below). Let us suppose its temperature is 17°C.

The air rises up the slopes. As a result, the pressure it is

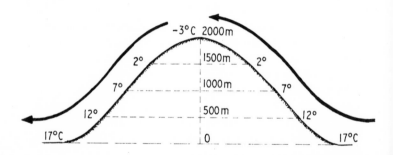

under decreases. The air is less 'compressed'; it expands. It will be realised that this *expansion* has a cooling effect (a fact that is easily checked by letting down a cycle tyre: the air, which expands as it escapes from the tyre, is colder than the surrounding air). This cooling is of the order of 1°C for each 100m. If the mountain is 2,000m high, the temperature of the air as it passes over the summit is therefore −3°C.

The air then descends on the other side. The pressure it is under increases. It compresses, and this compression makes it warmer. This heating process occurs at the same rate as the preceding cooling: 1°C per 100m. At the foot of the mountain, the air has recovered its former temperature: 17°C.

Three principles must be remembered from this example:

− As it rises the air has cooled, but it regains its original temperature at the end of its descent. The changes it has suffered have been counteractive: no loss or gain of heat. The variations of temperature of the moving air go on in *adiabatic* fashion, that is to say without heat exchange with the surrounding environment.
− The rate of variation of temperature of the moving air is 1°C per 100m, if this air only contains water in the vapour form. It is called the adiabatic gradient of unsaturated air, or more simply *dry adiabatic lapse rate* (DALR).
− It is seen that the vertical lapse rate of the moving air is clearly different from the vertical lapse rate of motionless air: 10°C per km instead of 6°C per km.

Second case

The air has the same temperature as in the preceding case: 17°C. It is still clear but this time it contains more water vapour.

As it rises it cools. At a certain height (let us say for instance, at 1,000m, where the temperature of the air is 7°C), suddenly something happens: everything becomes murky. We are witnessing the birth of a cloud. Why?

Because the air can only retain a limited amount of water

in the form of vapour, and the colder it is the less it can hold. The relationship between the quantity of water vapour that the air actually contains and the maximum amount it can contain for the same temperature, defines its *relative humidity*. This is expressed as a percentage. In our example, the quantity of water vapour that the air easily accepted at 17°C, becomes its maximum amount at 7°C. Its relative humidity is then in the order of 100 per cent. *Saturation* is reached. Should the air cool still further, the excess water vapour is transformed into microscopic droplets, kept in the air by the wind. There is then *condensation* (the change from the gaseous to the liquid state) which takes the form of cloud. This condensation frequently occurs only after some delay during which the air is in a state of *supersaturation*.

As its water vapour condenses, the air continues nevertheless to rise up the mountain. But, from the moment when the condensation occurs, its temperature decreases less quickly with the height. The condensation, in fact, frees heat (the same heat which had formerly brought about the evaporation of the water over the ocean; it is called *latent heat*). The variations in temperature now take place according to a different lapse rate, which is the saturated *pseudoadiabatic lapse rate* (pseudo, because there is an exchange of heat between the air and the water droplets or the ice crystals contained in the cloud) and which henceforward we shall call *saturated adiabatic lapse rate* (SALR). This rate can vary between 0.5°C and 0.8°C per 100m. We shall take it here as 0.6°C.

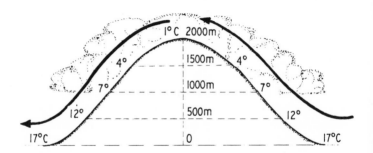

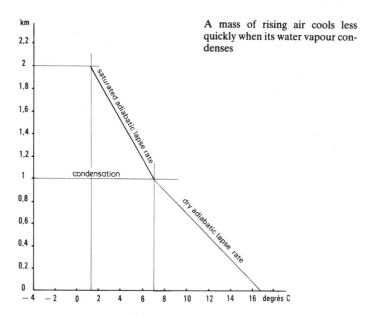

A mass of rising air cools less quickly when its water vapour condenses

At the top of the mountain, the air is therefore less cold than in the first case. It is at 1°C. As it descends, it is compressed, and heats up at a rate of 0.6°C per 100m. As it warms, the water droplets evaporate. At 1,000m altitude, the evaporation is complete and the air is again clear; in the ensuing descent, the temperature increases according to the dry adiabatic lapse rate. At the foot of the mountain, the air is again at 17°C.

Conclusions from this example:

– Condensation is due to the cooling of the air.
– As it rises, saturated air cools less quickly than clear air.

It should be noted at this point that the condensation of water vapour can occur as a result of cooling which does not only originate from the rising of the air. Cooling can be caused by radiation (as happens at night: the air radiates its heat and this radiation is no longer compensated for by the

21

sun's rays); and by contact with a cold surface (the bottle one takes out of the ice box is covered with mist). But in a free atmosphere, the most frequent cause of cooling, and therefore of condensation, is the expansion of the rising air we have just been describing.

Taking an overall view of the mountain, it is clear that the cloud that covers its summit has a very clear cut base, at 1,000m altitude. It does not move, although the wind is moving through it. In fact, it is never the same cloud; the water droplets which compose it are constantly being renewed.

The clouds which originate in free atmosphere have similar characteristics. Their base is often horizontal; in a given situation, clouds of the same origin all have their bases at the same height. And it can already be guessed that a cloud, even when it drifts with the wind, is not a stable, simple ball of cottonwool, but rather an agglomerate in a constant state of renewing its particles that are rising and falling, some condensing, others evaporating.

Third case

The air which approaches the mountain has still the same temperature, but this time it contains still more water vapour. The condensation of the latter occurs very quickly, at an altitude of 200m for example, and at a temperature therefore of 15°C. At the summit, the air is at 4.2°C.

But, in the course of the rise, another change has taken place: there has been *precipitation*. It has rained. Despite appearances, rain is a very complicated phenomenon, which we shall not even try to explain. If it has rained, the air has lost some of its water content – we shall leave it at that.

When it descends on the far slope, the air warms up according to the saturated adiabatic lapse rate. But it contains less water than before and there is a smaller number of droplets to evaporate. After 1,000m fall, for example, the temperature being 10.2°C, evaporation is complete. The heating process then continues according to the dry adiabatic

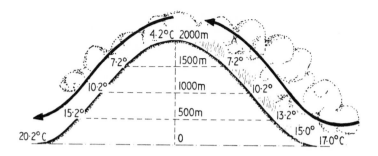

lapse rate, at 1°C per 100m. At the foot of the mountain, the air is at 20.2°C. In other words, after its passage over the mountain, the air is warmer than it was before (this phenomenon is known to meteorologists as *Föhn effect*). The heat freed by the condensation is only partially reabsorbed by the evaporation; the 'excess' contributes to increasing the temperature of the air. The simple conclusion is that by losing water, the air has warmed up.

Fourth case

In the preceding examples, the wind was hot. Now imagine it is much colder: the air approaching the mountain is at 6°C.

Condensation occurs, for example, at a height of 300m. The air is then at 3°C. Its temperature, decreasing subsequently according to the saturated adiabatic lapse rate, is at 0° at 800m. One might then expect the water droplets composing the cloud were going to change into ice; but this is not always the case. It is often found that this change takes place in phases, and is only completed at a temperature around −40°C. The droplets of water that remain thus in a liquid state below 0°C are said to be in a state of *supercooling*.

This can be disconcerting. A motorist crossing the mountain, when he arrives at an altitude where the temperature is below 0°C, is annoyed when his windscreen frosts over. In fact a slight impact or the presence of impurities in the air is enough to change the supercooled droplets instantly into ice; this is the sole cause of freezing fog.

To complete our survey of the possible air changes, we repeat that when it is very cold its water vapour content is changed directly into ice, without passing through the liquid state (*deposition*); similarly and conversely, it changes directly from the solid state to the gaseous one. This phenomenon is called *sublimation*.

Clouds composed of ice crystals appear at high altitude (usually above 6,000m). They are easily recognisable by their silky, dazzling-white appearance. Clouds composed of water droplets are greyer, nor are they so high, but they can exist at heights with temperatures well below 0°C.

Now that we have acquired these basic facts we shall leave the mountains. This account of the changes that occur in air as it rises and falls has supplied the fundamental facts for understanding the other part of the story, which is an infinitely more complicated and tortuous one, about the air masses that circulate in free atmosphere, and whose twists and turns create weather.

The air masses

The principal characteristic of the atmosphere is unquestionably its sensitivity to influences. When, for example, parcels of air have remained for a time on one geographic area, they finally acquire similar characteristics: the same humidity and temperature. They can form a homogenous whole or *air mass*. So it is that we can speak of warm air masses and cold air masses, damp air masses and dry air masses, tropical air masses and polar air masses. The volume of these masses is very variable: they can extend over a few hundreds or over several thousands of kilometres and be several hundreds or some thousands of metres thick.

An air mass is characterised in the first place by its place of origin. But as we have said, air masses travel and it follows that in the course of their journey they are influenced by the regions they cross, and that their characteristics change with conditions. They can be transformed.

To put a recognisable label on these air masses, two concepts must be grasped. One concerns their temperature: what do we call a warm air mass, a cold air mass, what do we mean by 'heat' and 'cold'? The other is about what is best described as their temperament. There are masses of stable and unstable air. What is the difference? When one goes sailing, one soon finds out.

Warm air, cold air

The sensations of hot and cold, as we experience them, are relative and the terms 'hotter' and 'colder', even more so. In fact, the human body is rather insensitive to small changes in temperature, but much more so to variations in the relative humidity of the air. So, when a mass of very damp air arrives, there can be an impression of cold, even when the temperature is in fact rising, for damp air takes more calories out of us than dry air.

In any case, when it comes to determining the temperature of the air mass invading our immediate environment, our sensory impressions, even when correct, prove to be inadequate; the idea of hot and cold, in meteorological terms, is on quite another scale.

To understand this, let us return for a moment to the first case in our recent example – air passing, without condensation, over the mountain. If two parcels of this air are compared, taken at different altitudes, one at 400m, for instance, as it rises, the other at 1,500m as it descends, they are found not to have the same temperature; one is at 13°C, the other at 2°C. However, we know that the air, after crossing the mountain, returns to the temperature it had when it approached its foot. Can it be that one of these parcels is hotter than the other? In fact, in order to compare them effectively, we must, by calculation (taking into account the adiabatic process), bring them both to the same pressure. It is only then their temperature is the same.

It is the same with the second case we cited, when condensation occurred. By contrast, in the third case where the air loses part of its moisture on the way, if two particles of air are compared, one before precipitation, the other after, it will be found that they are different: under the same pressure, one is actually hotter than the other.

In short, when warm air rises it can reach a very low temperature but nevertheless it remains warm air. The arrival of a warm air mass can thus be forecast (as often happens) by the appearance of clouds solely composed of ice crystals.

Observations taken vertically through the atmosphere reveal the temperature and moisture content of the air at given altitudes. Through bringing, by calculation, different particles of air to the same pressure, the so-called *reference pressure* (conventionally 1,000mb), meteorologists can know what sort of air masses they are dealing with.

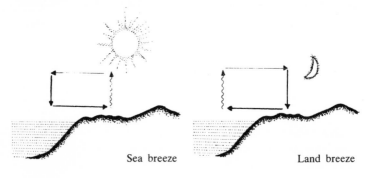

Sea breeze   Land breeze

Land and sea breezes

The behaviour of warm air and cold air in relation to each other depends essentially on their different densities. Warm air is lighter, cold air heavier. The warm air tends to rise, the cold air to descend and spread out.

A typical example of their relationship is provided by the phenomenon of land and sea breezes, frequently to be observed on the coast during periods of fine weather.

This phenomenon is bound to a fundamental fact: the land and the sea have very different thermal properties. The land warms and cools very quickly; the sea, in contrast, is subject to slow variations of temperature.

In the day time, the land warms under the heat of the sun, heats the air above it, and this warm air tends to rise. The colder air over the sea tends to spread and fill the vacuum left by the warm air. The wind then blows from the sea towards the land.

At night, the land cools. The sea is warmer (or less cold). The wind now blows from the land towards the sea.

Warm air and cold air, in brief, organise themselves into a kind of vertical circuit: the warm air rises, the cold air takes its place and is heated in turn. The warm air, which has risen, cools and comes down again to take the place abandoned by the cold air. This is the principle of convection of which we have already spoken.

It is important to know that, owing to their different densities, warm air and cold air mix no better than oil and water. The behaviour of coastal breezes is on the whole better organised; but, on quite another scale: when warm air and cold air masses meet, it doesn't happen without a clash, as we shall see.

Stable and unstable air

Vertical movements can occur in the very heart of an air mass as a result of influences around it. Sometimes these movements are quickly subdued and the air mass is designated *stable*. In other cases the influence is considerable and the air mass is then *unstable*.

Take a mass of clear air with a vertical thermal environmental lapse rate (the rate of decrease of temprature with height) of 0.5°C per 100m, that is to say less than the dry adiabatic lapse rate. Under the effect of some impulse, a parcel of this mass gains 100m in height. Its temperature decreases according to the dry adiabatic lapse rate of 1°C. It is colder, therefore heavier, than the surrounding air and it tends to fall. In the same conditions, a parcel of air falling by 100m is warmer, therefore lighter, than the surrounding air

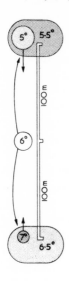

◀ The enviromental lapse rate of the air mass (0.5°C per 100m) is less than the adiabatic lapse rate: the air is stable

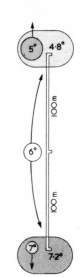

The enviromental lapse rate of the ▶ air mass (1.2°C per 100m) is higher than the adiabatic lapse rate: the air is unstable

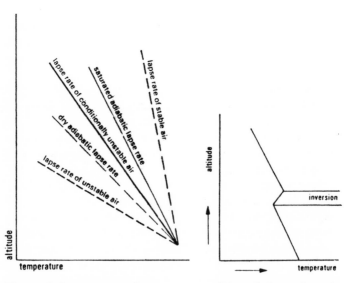

The vertical temperature lapse rate of an air mass determines its degree of stability or instability

Warmed from above or cooled from below, the air becomes stable and it tends to rise again. The air mass under consideration is stable.

If it is a saturated air mass, the variations of temperature occur according to the saturated adiabatic lapse rate, but the result is the same.

Let us now take an air mass with a greater vertical thermal environmental lapse rate of 1.2°C for instance. A parcel of air rising 100m cools by only 1°C: it is then warmer than the surrounding air and it has therefore a tendency to continue rising. On the contrary, a parcel falling by 100m is colder than the surrounding air: it tends to continue falling. The air mass is traversed by vertical movements, which make its interior remarkably turbulent. It is therefore unstable.

It is seen therefore that the degree of stability or instability of an air mass depends on the relationship between the vertical thermal environmental lapse rate of the air in question and the adiabatic lapse rates. Two particular cases must be considered:

1   The environmental lapse rate of the air mass is equal to the adiabatic lapse rate (dry in the case of a mass of clear air, saturated in the case of a mass of saturated air): this air mass is in *neutral equilibrium*.
2   The vertical thermal environmental lapse rate lies between the two adiabatic lapse rates. As long as the air remains clear, the air mass is stable. But if, for any reason (total rise of the mass, for instance), condensation occurs, the air mass becomes unstable. This type of air mass is termed *conditionally unstable*.

From these different observations, it can be deduced:

– Everything that tends to increase the vertical thermal environmental lapse rate of an air mass (heating from below, or cooling from above) tends to render that air mass unstable.
– Everything tending to reduce its vertical thermal environmental lapse rate (cooling from below, heating from above) tends to make it stable.

Naturally, if the temperature increases with the altitude instead of decreasing, the environmental lapse rate being inverted, there is total stability. This is the case in the stratosphere. These *temperature inversions* also occur in the troposphere, when a mass of warm air passes over the top of a mass of cold air. The layer where the inversion occurs blocks off all rising movements, as if it were a tight lid closing off all vertical exchanges.

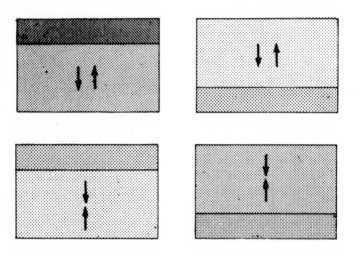

Cooled from above or warmed from below, the air becomes unstable

At our level, the stability or instability of an air mass is given concrete form by the sort of wind that springs from it. A mass of stable air gives winds that can be strong but steady. In a mass of unstable air, on the contrary, the wind is variable, often blowing in gusty squalls. That is the time to keep your weather eye open.

But there exists a much more precise method of identifying the air masses. All one needs do is to lift the eyes and look up at the sky. The air movements are revealed, in the clearest possible way, by the clouds.

Clouds

A mass of unstable air is shown up by rounded masses of cloud heaped on each other. Generally well separated from each other, sometimes with marked vertical development, these clouds demonstrate intense convective activity in the atmosphere. They are *cumulus* or *cumuliform* clouds.

Often they can be seen climbing into the sky, during fine weather at the hottest hour of the day. They sometimes form up in line, over the coast, reproducing its outline exactly (revealing, at sea, the presence of a distant island). The appearance of these cumuli is comparable with the routine of land and sea breezes, mentioned above. It reveals the existence of rising currents above overheated land; the air cools as it rises, condenses and forms these clouds, separated from one another by stretches of blue sky which conceal descending currents. Very often the sky is heavy over the coast, while it is perfectly clear at sea. The air above the land is unstable, the air above the sea is stable. If you want to take advantage of the sun, now is the time to get under way (but if you want to profit from it to the very last ray, you will come home with the wind on your nose).

In a mass of stable air, these convection movements do not occur; this type of cloud never appears. When condensation occurs it is due to a general cooling of the air mass. The clouds which result spread out in a uniform layer, never very thick, which often covers a larger area. They are generally grey and are the *stratus* type (*stratiform* clouds).

Both categories of clouds are sometimes associated, the cumulus gather in groups, in round or rocklike shapes that rise like mountainous towers according to the altitude. Such clouds usually denote some instability and turbulence along the demarcation line between two different air masses.

Of course clouds defy, in hundreds of minor ways, this rather rough classification. It is usually very difficult to know their precise significance. Familiarity with clouds takes as long to acquire as familiarity with the wind that drives our

31

boats along. It takes patient study, done in a mood of contemplation and a distrust of categorical assertions. Some would call it daydreaming, being unaware how fruitful daydreaming can be!

Officially, clouds are divided into ten different *types*. This classification takes into account both their shape and the height at which they appear. The troposphere, the region of the clouds, is then divided into three layers. A cloud's name indicates both its structure and the layer where it lies:

- The cirrus, cirrocumulus and cirrostratus belong to the upper layer; they appear between altitudes of 6 and 13km in northern latitudes, and are composed of ice crystals.
- The altocumulus and altostratus are the middle layer clouds (between 2 and 7km high). They are composed mainly of water droplets.
- The stratocumulus and stratus are found in the lowest layer between the Earth's surface and a height of 2km.

But this classification is a little too precise: three types of cloud lie outside it. These are the clouds with vertical development which can occupy several layers at the same time: nimbostratus, cumulus, and especially the enormous cumulonimbus.

To describe the ten cloud types, we will keep to our original three classifications: clouds of instability, of limited instability and of stability – taking into account the concept of layers.

Clouds of instability

Cumulus (Cu). Clouds separated from each other, with clear outlines, with quite considerable vertical development. Their base is often horizontal and their summits often take the form of protuberances in the shape of towers and domes, sometimes burgeoning not unlike cauliflower curds.

Cumulus form in all sizes. The smallest ones are often the result of a very localised warming of the ground: a cumulus

Cumulus (humilis) ▲

▼ Cumulonimbus

can even form over a cornfield, which is clearly hotter than a small copse nearby. This is the cumulus *humilis*, the little clouds typically seen scattered along the coast. This is the outstanding fine weather cloud. It means no rain.

Larger cumulus, cumulus *mediocris*, or cumulus *congestus*, invades large areas of sky and can indicate the arrival of a mass of cold air, which heats on contacting the land and therefore becomes unstable. The base of heavy cumulus is usually dark with summits blinding white in the sun. A cumulus *congestus* can be several kilometres in diameter and as thick as 5,000m. The tall towers it thrusts up into the sky characterise it clearly. It sometimes brings showers but especially violent squalls of wind.

Cumulonimbus (Cb). King of the clouds, the cumulonimbus is a cumulus *congestus* that has grown out of all proportion. Its depth varies from 5m to 12,000m. Its top is made up of ice crystals and often spreads out in the form of an anvil, to the limit of the stratosphere. It marks the existence of extremely powerful, ascending air currents, and produces violent showers of rain, hail or snow, and thunder storms. Below such a cloud, the wind blows at gale force, in unpredictable directions.

Clouds of limited instability

Cirrocumulus (Cc). Small clouds of the upper layer, very white and shiny, without shadow. They assemble in banks or ridges, regularly distributed like fish scales (hence the term 'mackerel sky') usually against a very blue sky. Each unit has a width apparently less than 1° (i.e. it is concealed behind a little finger held at arm's length).

Altocumulus (Ac). Clouds of the middle layer, with the same kind of organisation pattern as the cirrocumulus, but with larger components (three fingers are needed to cover them). They are composed of rounded masses with a wavy appearance, white or grey, or both white and grey at the same time. They are fairly thick and more or less fused together. The sun can often be seen through them. They are the clouds of the French proverb: a mackerel sky and a powdered woman don't last long.

The altocumulus are very frequently seen. They can be observed forming simultaneously at different levels (between 1,500 and 5,000m). When they have a stormy character, they can become very thick and yet remain quite clear.

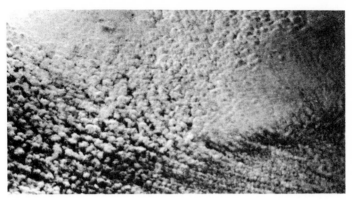

Cirrocumulus ▲

▼ Altocumulus

Stratocumulus (Sc). Clouds of the lowest layer, which arise in banks or sheets. They are grey or whitish, or both, at the same time and almost always have dark parts. Their components look like broad slabs or pebbles and have often a thick wavy appearance. They can fuse together and cover the whole sky overhead, their wavy forms only revealed by shades of grey. They bring drizzle rather than rain.

Stratocumulus ▲

▼ Cirrus

Clouds of stability

Cirrus (Ci). Clouds of the upper layer, the cirrus are quite different from the other clouds in a stable weather pattern. They are isolated clouds, white threads or 'mares' tails' like claw marks on the sky. Composed solely of ice crystals, they are shiny, have neither a shadow of their own nor a projected shadow. The forms they take often denote the presence of strong wind at high altitude.

Cirrostratus

Cirrostratus (Cs) is a thin, transparent cloud that forms a veil over the sky. Smooth or fibrous, it often succeeds the cirrus. The blue of the sky pales, but the sun shines virtually as brightly. So tenuous is the cloud that it is often only disclosed by the sight of the haloes that it produces round the sun or moon. A halo 22° wide is said to be measurable by holding your hand straight out at arm's length towards the sun so that it is at your finger tips.

Altostratus (As) has a thicker veil-like appearance and appears lower down than the cirrostratus, to which it often succeeds. It is a greyish or bluish colour, furrowed or smooth, and covers the sky partially or entirely. The sun still penetrates it as if it were shining through frosted glass. It all looks innocent enough but at sea it can still burn you very badly.

The altostratus can thicken, become very grey and bring a few drops of rain.

Nimbostratus (Ns) is a thick cloudy grey layer, often very dark, which spreads over the whole sky, and usually follows

37

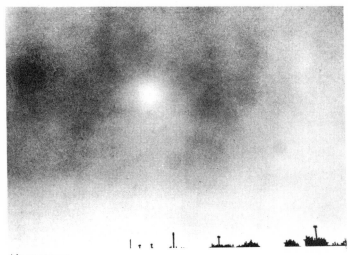

Altostratus ▲

▼ Nimbostratus

a thick veil of altostratus. Its outlines are blurred by continual precipitations. Small black ragged clouds frequently run beneath it.

It darkens the sky and lights must be turned on. The nimbostratus is the cloud that brings interminable rain (or snow). It can be 5,000m thick and extend over hundreds of miles.

Stratus (St). A very low cloud, of uniform grey, it is often quite clear. Sometimes the outline of the sun can be seen clearly through it. It can cover the whole sky or else trail over the sea in jagged banks. It is often the result of fog which has risen slightly up from the ground. It can produce drizzle, hail or granulated snow.

The succession, cirrus, cirrostratus, altostratus, nimbostratus, stratocumulus (and sometimes stratus), is a classic one in northern latitudes. It heralds, as we shall see in the next chapter, the arrival of a warm air mass, like the advance guard rattling along the heights while the main body of the troops follow at sea level.

Stratus

Fogs

The meteorologists speak of *fog* when visibility at ground level is below 1km; of *mist* when it is between 1 and 2km. Sailors refer to fog, whatever visibility it allows. There is some terminological inexactitude in weather descriptions.

The fog and mists met with at sea are closely associated with the phenomena of advection and radiation.

Advection fog is the most common type at sea. Advection – in contrast with convection – is displacement of air horizontally. Advection fog arises from condensation occurring in a mass of warm, damp air passing over a cold surface. This sort of fog is almost permanent over the Newfoundland Banks where the air, warmed and saturated with humidity over the Gulf Stream, meets the cold Labrador Current. Generally speaking, the higher the latitude, the colder the sea, and the more frequently is this type of fog met. It is commoner in winter than in summer. In France, it is particularly prevalent in areas with strong currents, like the Raz de Sein, the Four Channel on the north-west coast and the Raz Blanchard for instance. The turbulence that occurs in a swift tidal stream brings cold water up to the surface.

Radiation fog is essentially a land fog that occurs in clear, calm weather. During the night, the Earth loses its heat by radiation, the air in contact with it cools and the water vapour it contains condenses. This fog is particularly dense at first light, the coldest hour. It lingers sometimes for a long time on low ground where the cold air tends to gather. It occurs in estuaries and sometimes spills over a little out to sea, obscuring the coastal lights.

Classification of the air masses

With practice, one succeeds in identifying the various cloud types at a glance. But the precise identification of the air mass in which it lies needs the application of other senses than sight – touch and smell itself because the air masses can pick up the smells of the regions they have passed through.

We know for a fact that air masses are characterised by their origins and their journeyings. This is how air masses from the Arctic, the North Pole, the tropics or the equator, be they maritime or continental, can be distinguished.

Arctic air. Coming from the polar icecap, Arctic air is, at the outset, cold, dry, and stable. Moving towards more temperate latitudes, it becomes laden with moisture over the sea and heated from below and becomes unstable. Sometimes, around Iceland, it finds a path down which it tracks straight down to north-west Europe. The weather is then very cold, and the sky is a pale, very characteristic, emerald green, with many cumulus and cumulonimbus. Thunder storms are frequent, squalls violent, winds strong. Between squalls, visibility is excellent.

Polar air. The polar maritime air is usually Arctic air that has not succeeded in escaping and that has hung around a long time in the sub-polar regions (between 60° and 70° latitude). It has absorbed its moisture gradually, and has become progressively warm. When it arrives in the English Channel area, as it commonly does, this polar maritime air is unstable, but less so than the Arctic air. The cumuliform clouds are not so numerous, the squalls not so violent. Visibility is still excellent.

The polar continental air is Arctic air that has made a detour over the continents. Its characteristics vary according to the seasons, and the nature of the ground it has passed over. It is stable in winter, sometimes unstable in summer. When it arrives in western Europe from Russia, it gives dry cold weather with a cloudless sky in winter; in summer, fine, rather cloudy weather.

Tropical air. Tropical maritime air, coming out of the subtropical regions (between 30° and 40° latitude), is warm and laden with moisture, unstable from the outset. As it reaches temperate latitudes, it is cooled from the base and tends to become stable. Its arrival in western Europe is often signalled by the famous succession of stratiform clouds that we have mentioned above. Sometimes this maritime tropical air is still unstable on arrival and this is characterised by severe thunderstorms.

Tropical continental air, originating in North Africa or the Near East, is very dry and stable when it sets out, and cannot create clouds. But as it passes over the Mediterranean or the Atlantic, it becomes laden with moisture. Its arrival in Europe, in summer, brings very hot weather and violent storms over high ground.

Equatorial air is very hot, very damp and very unstable. It contributes to the formation of tropical cyclones. It rarely reaches France and the United Kingdom but when it does arrive it gives rise to very violent disturbances.

The air masses have not always got the clear-cut characteristics we have just given and, in any case, there is no consistently uniform air mass, be it polar or tropical, but many and varied masses of air have a polar or tropical origin. They develop and circulate at different rates; they warm up, cool down, become moist or dry, or more stable or less stable, as their wanderings take them. The essential fact to grasp is that when two air masses of different temperature (and therefore of different density) meet, they do not mix: they clash. The area where the confrontation takes place is called the *frontal zone* and its track over the ground a *front*.

The principal fronts are:

– The Arctic front, separating the masses of Arctic air from the masses of polar air;
– The polar front, separating the masses of polar air from the masses of tropical air;
– The inter-tropical front, a zone of convergences for the winds of the two hemispheres.

We shall have good reasons for reverting to the polar front in the next chapter.

Wind

Our study of the behaviour of moving air and of the different types of air masses travelling over the globe eventually drew attention to the wind and some of its local manifestations. It is now time to examine winds without attempting to get involved too deeply in scientific phenomena. What is wind? Why does it blow in one direction rather than another? Why does it vary in strength?

The answer lies first in a reconsideration of atmospheric pressure, that has just been referred to in connection with the phenomenon of expansion. It has been made clear that atmospheric pressure is closely connected with temperature, cold air being heavier than warm air and the weight of an air column at a given spot depending on the temperature of the air itself. In addition to the thermal factor there are the dynamic ones – the rotation of the Earth and movements of air masses. It has also become clear that pressure can vary considerably from hour to hour within the same area, and it follows logically enough that it varies from one place to another.

The comparison of pressures taken at different points on the Earth's surface is one of the keys to meteorology. To make this comparison, all measurements are first of all reduced to the same reference point, which is sea level. The results obtained are then charted and all points with equal pressure are joined together. These lines of equal pressure are called *isobars*. Drawn usually at intervals of 5 millibars, they disclose the equivalent of a relief map of the atmosphere, just as contour lines on survey maps show land contours, and surroundings on charts indicate least depth.

The outlines of the isobars outline various shapes on the maps – the so-called isobaric shapes – which illustrate the characteristic movements of the air masses. It will be noticed that in certain areas the isobars are circular and fit more or less regularly into one another. When the height of the isobars decreases towards the centre of the shape, in the outline of a bowl, there is an *area of low pressure*, or a *depression*. Conversely, when the height of the isobars increases as they approach the centre, forming a 'hill', there is an *area of high pressure*, or *anti-cyclone*.

There are also other shapes outlined on the weather charts:

– 'Valleys' that extend the depressions between areas of high pressure are known as *troughs*;
– 'Promontories', projecting the anticyclones into a depression, are *ridges*;
– Areas of relatively low pressure, connecting two depressions (or two highs), are *cols*;

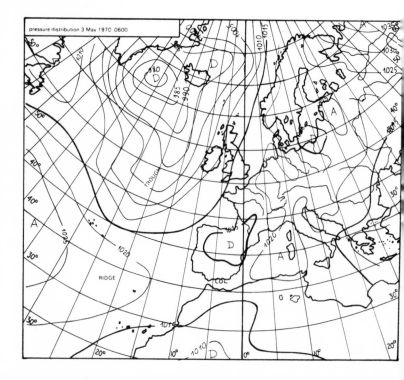

– Areas with contours showing pressures not much different from the average pressure are called *barometric fens* in France.

Winds result from the differences in atmospheric pressures shown on the map. It would all be much easier if a simple definition were possible. Wind is air moving from high pressure towards low pressure areas, like air escaping from a tyre or a ball rolling down a slope. Unfortunately, that is only a half-truth.

Direction of the wind

A ball, released at the top of a hill, rolls in the direction of the steepest slope. One might think it would be the same with air and that the wind direction would be at right angles to the isobars. This would no doubt be the case if the Earth were motionless, and if it were a perfectly smooth globe. But the Earth turns perpetually and is, moreover, not upright.

Because the Earth is rotating, all moving bodies on its surface are exposed to a deflecting force, called the *Coriolis Force*, which acts at right angles to the direction of the movement. Observation shows that, in the northern hemisphere, all trajectories are deflected to the right, whatever their direction, and that they are deflected to the left in the southern hemisphere.* Thus, the Gulf Stream, as it moves north, curves away towards the east; the Labrador Current, descending in the opposite direction, is flattened against the American continental barrier.

On land, on very busy railway tracks, a micrometer demonstrates that the right hand rail is always more worn

*This is a fundamental fact, and it can be stated once and for all that all movements of atmosphere in the southern hemisphere go in the opposite direction to the northern one. We shall only speak here of the northern hemisphere.

For the convenience of the reader who adventures into southern waters and who will read this chapter upside down.

than the left hand one. Fortunately the Coriolis Force is very weak and is not felt by human beings when they move, but it has as much influence on the wind as the pressure force.

In anticyclones, air tends to move outwards from the centre towards the circumference. Deflected to the right, it therefore moves in a clockwise direction. But in depressions, the air tends to move from the circumference towards the centre and, still deflected to the right, it therefore moves in an anti-clockwise direction.

A practical observation follows from this law *(The law of Buys-Ballot)*, that an observer facing the wind always has low pressure on his right and high pressure on his left.

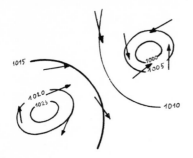

Buys-Ballot's law

northern hemisphere

southern hemisphere

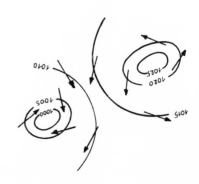

That is the main principle, but there are important variations because the wind blows in different directions high up and at ground level.

At heights, two forces determine direction: the pressure force, directed from high towards low pressure, and the Coriolis Force which deflects the air towards the right. They balance each other out in such a way that the wind blows parallel to the isobars.

Near the ground, friction intervenes. Its action is proportional to the unevenness of the surface. It modifies the relationship of the forces in such a way that the air, at ground level, is deflected less towards the right than it is high up. So it can be said that the wind has a tendency to 'move out' of anticyclones, and to 'move into' depressions. At sea, the angle it makes with the isobars is, on average, of the order of 30°.

The difference of direction between wind at height and wind on ground level explains a phenomenon which can be often observed at sea, in squally weather. When an observer, standing facing the wind, sees a squall coming straight at him, he eventually remarks that the squall passes to his left. But it is the squall coming a little from his right that he ought to keep an eye on.

Let us suppose that the wind is constant, eg that the parcels of air are all moving at a constant speed. In this case, the forces acting on these parcels are balanced.

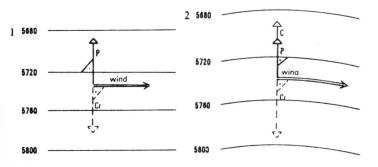

1 *High altitude wind (more than 2,000m) parallel straight iso-bars.* If there is to be a balance of forces, Cr (Coriolis Force), which is at right angles to the wind, must be equal and opposite to P (pressure force) which is also at right angles to the isobars and the further apart they are, the gentler the wind. This is the *geostrophic wind*; its scale is given on met maps and allows an evaluation of the ground wind speed to be made.

2 *High altitude wind, curved isobars.* For a balance of forces, Cr which is at right angles to the wind must be equal: to P+C (centrifugal force) in an anticyclone; to P−C in a depression. P is at right angles to the isobars. C is at right angles to the wind, therefore parallel to P; concurrent with P in an anticyclone, opposed to P in a depression. This wind is called the *gradient wind*.

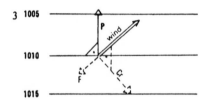

3 *Ground wind, straight isobars.* The three forces must balance out. P is at right angles to the isobars. Cr is at right angles to the wind. F (friction) is opposed to the wind (or at right angles to Cr). The greater F is, the more the wind will approach the direction of P. This wind is equal to about 0.8×the geostrophic wind.

4–5 *Ground wind, curved isobars.* The four forces must balance. P is at right angles to the isobars. Cr is at right angles to the wind. C is at right angles to the wind. F is opposed to the wind (or at right angles to Cr). This wind is also equal to 0.8×the geostrophic wind.

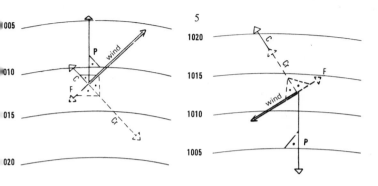

Wind speed

The speed of the wind is directly linked to the *pressure gradient*, represented on the maps by the spacing of the isobars. The closer the isobars are together, the steeper the gradient, the stronger the wind. In our latitudes, isobars spaced out at some 100km apart indicate winds of approximately 100km an hour.

It will be noticed that the isobars in anticyclones are usually well spaced out: the winds are weak. Around depressions on the contrary, the isobars are often very close together and therefore indicate violent winds.

Let us note finally that, because of friction, wind at ground level is considerably less strong than at heights. Even a few metres from the ground, the difference is perceptible (in the order of 10 per cent for the first ten metres). This percentage mounts increasingly the higher up the wind is blowing.

General circulation

Normal weather maps, which give the average pressures on the globe's surface in winter and summer, bring out the fact that, between equator and the poles in both hemispheres, there is an alternation of high pressure and low pressure zones:

– Low pressure at the equator;
– High pressure in the tropics;
– Low pressure in the temperate regions;
– High pressure at the poles.

By applying the Buys-Ballot law, it is easy to understand now why the average winds at ground level should be easterly and westerly, and we find:

– Easterlies predominating in the tropical regions (the *tradewinds*);
– Westerlies predominating in the temperate regions;
– Easterlies predominating in the polar regions.

The two calm zones are at the equator (the region where the gradient of pressure is weak – the *doldrums*) and in the tropics (calm sunny zones of high pressure).

This pattern is not absolutely regular. The uneven heating of the oceans and continents, seasonal variations and the appearance of 'disturbances' in the temperate zones all contribute to variations and the breaking up of these pressure belts. The winds come as a consequence of them.

A concrete picture of the average circulation of air streams in summer and winter is given on the maps opposite.

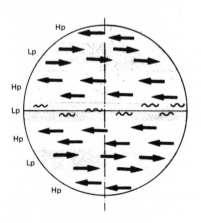

Lp: low pressure
Hp: high pressure

A. Normal wind directions and action centres in July

B. Normal wind directions and action centres in January

A number of eddies (vortices) will be immediately noticeable. They correspond to anticyclones and depressions of a permanent or semi-permanent type which are called *action centres*.

The large swirls which appear in the Pacific and the Atlantic (their distribution is impressively symmetrical) are anticyclones of dynamic origin which is a symptom of the rotation of the Earth. From one season to the next, they move only slightly and their configuration does not change. They are *permanent* action centres. The North Atlantic anticyclone, the one which particularly interests us, is called the *Azores anticyclone*. This is the one which pushes the masses of Tropical maritime air (Tm) towards our latitudes.

More difficult to distinguish, but no less important, are the depressions situated between 60° and 70° north, between the east winds of the polar ice cap and the west winds of the temperate regions: to the north of the Aleutians, to the west of Greenland, to the south of Iceland. These too are also permanent centres of action of dynamic origin. It will be noticed besides how much these anticyclones and depressions are linked: the Aleutian depression is situated to the north-east of the North Pacific anticyclone; the Icelandic depression to the north-east of the Azores anticyclone. This Icelandic depression, it will again be noticed, is more accentuated in winter than in summer and many yachtsmen exploit this as an argument for staying indoors at this time of the year.

On continents, variations are much more clear-cut from one season to the next. They are linked to the great temperature variations to which the land is subject. The case of the Asian continent is particularly noteworthy. In winter with

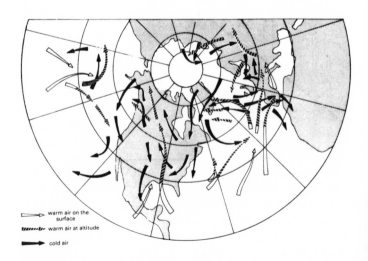

Example of the general circulation of air masses between the Tropics and the Polar regions (7 May 1933)

the ground cooling, high pressure areas are established and an anticyclone is formed: the winds move outwards towards the oceans. In summer, the ground is overheated and the anticyclone is replaced by a vast zone of low pressure. The winds then move inland from the oceans to the interior and the rainy season begins. This phenomenon is familiar the world over as the *monsoon*. The anticyclones and depressions which are formed in this way on the continents therefore have a thermal origin. They are *seasonal action centres* of which Eurasian anticyclones are typical.

This general picture of the circulation of air masses does not exactly explain how heat transfers occur between the equator and the poles, and an explanation has still to be found. An examination of *synoptic* charts (which give an overall picture) shows that air masses become detached from time to time from the polar ice cap and make their way towards the equator. To compensate for this movement, warm air masses leave the equator for the north. The Coriolis Force deviates all the movements towards the right and it is likely that none of them ever reaches its destination and that the heat transfer takes place in stages. A mass of equatorial air, for instance, that arrives at latitude 45°, continues to be subject to the Coriolis Force, and so tends to return southwards. But at the top of its curve this air mass has lost heat and it has therefore become a cooling agent on its return to the hot areas where it originated. The same process may well be repeated from one area to another. Perhaps this is how it happens – or there may be some other explanation.

No doubt the disturbances which take place inside these great air movements (extra-tropical depressions, tropical cyclones, waterspouts, thunder storms and tornadoes) also play a part in establishing the Earth's thermal balance but there are too many unknown factors for it to be possible to be certain of their role in the system.

The wind and the sea

The similarity between atmosphere circulation and oceanic surface currents may seem remarkable but it is natural enough as the same influences are at work in air and sea movements. We have already drawn attention earlier in this chapter to the activity of the great ocean streams which influence the thermal exchanges between the equator and the poles. An examination of an ocean current chart makes it clear that the similarity is very extensive. The direction of the rotation of the Gulf Stream corresponds exactly to the rotation of the winds around the Azores anticyclone; and the Labrador or the Aleutian cold currents to the currents of cold air coming from the poles. In some areas seasonal currents set in rhythm with the monsoons.

To these so-called *density* currents must be added *drift* currents, which are caused by the wind and which behave in exactly the same way as the wind itself.

This is not the book to cover all the essential points of the foregoing description of the ocean currents for it would be too detailed to be of any practical use for yachtsmen. The great atmospheric migrations are a different matter, since they run after us and create our daily weather, while we, who sail over relatively tiny areas of sea, do not need an overall picture of ocean currents to plan tomorrow's cruise.

What is of enormous interest, though, is a particular point in the relationships between the atmosphere and the oceans: how wind and sea react when they meet in the area where we are sailing and the adjacent areas; what happens when the two elements are extreme, especially when the wind is strong.

Waves

When the wind blows over a calm sea, the friction of the air raises ripples on the water. These can be quite transitory, but if the wind continues, undulations or wavelets form, then waves running over the water in the direction of the wind.

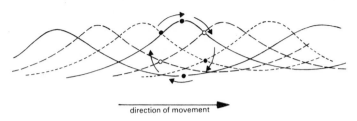

direction of movement

In spite of appearances, the water does not move: the cork returns to the same spot in relation to the bottom after the wave has passed

With rather less violence, the wind has the same effect on the sea as a paving stone thrown in to a pond: it makes a series of waves, and it is to be remembered that it is the waves that move, not the water itself. The liquid particles merely move orbitally, without changing position appreciably, as each undulation rolls by. The principle of this movement is demonstrated by watching a cork bobbing about on the water; when the wave arrives, the cork rises on the slope and moves a little forward; then, once the crest has passed, it moves downwards and backwards until it finally returns almost to its point of departure. Something of this movement is felt on board a boat running before the waves, when these are large enough: the boat accelerates on the forward slope of the wave, then seems, quite perceptibly, to be braked on the rear slope. Waves do not correspond to the horizontal movement of the water which the eye seems to see.

A wave can be defined first of all by its dimensions: its *height*, the vertical distance between the top of the crest and the bottom of the trough; its *length*, the distance between two troughs or between two crests (it is quite precise to talk of wave length). The relationship between a wave's height and length is its curve or steepness. A wave is always much longer than it is high; its steepness becomes critical when the ratio between height and length is in the order of 1:13. If the height increases any further, the waves *break* and then there really is a displacement of water in a horizontal direction.

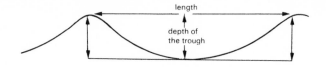

A wave is also defined by the *depth* to which its movement penetrates. Its depth is believed to be equal to its length, but in fact the movement is already very reduced at a depth equal to 1:9 of its length.

A wave, in fact, moves as part of a system of waves, which has its own rhythm, characterised by its frequency – the time which elapses between the passage of two crests at a given spot – and by its velocity, or the distance covered by a wave in a given time.

Clearly there exists a direct relationship between the length of the waves and the characteristics of the system of waves. This length (L) is equal to the product of the frequency (F) multiplied by the velocity (V): L=FV.

These definitions may be a little dry (and they are the only dry thing about them), but we shall see them come to life in the description of the principal characteristics the sea can assume wherever one happens to be.

We speak of a sea or sea condition to define any pattern of waves arising locally owing to the actual wind. We speak of *swell* when, in contrast, we see waves appearing, coming from a long way off, as a result of a wind which has blown (or is still blowing) somewhere else.

How waves originate

Let us suppose that the wind begins to blow, on a calm sea, in an area where you happen to be. The size of the waves which are going to develop depends on three factors:

– the strength of the wind
– how long it blows

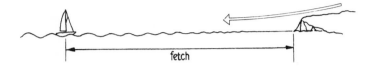

—its *fetch*, that is the distance over which the wind can exert
its effect without meeting any obstacles, or without changing direction itself.

The developing waves gradually gain height. At first they
have a very steep curve as their velocity is still low in proportion to the speed of the wind. If the wind continues, they
gradually get longer. Height, length, frequency and velocity
increase progressively to their maximum, according to the
strength of the wind. It can then go on blowing for days, but,
if its strength does not change, neither will the character of
the waves it has created alter.

But if the fetch is too short, they cannot reach their
optimum shape. When the first waves that developed, where

The distance over which the
wind blows, its 'fetch', can
alter

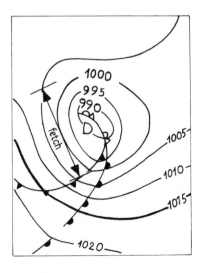

the wind began to blow, reach the end of the fetch (at the coast for instance), a balance is set up. Here again, the duration of the wind is of no importance, provided it continues to blow at the same strength. It follows that the shorter the fetch, the less chance the waves have of becoming big. It does not follow that sailing is necessarily any pleasanter in a small enclosed sea than right out in the ocean, for the waves cannot space out, but remain short and steep and the boat pounds harder than on a well formed sea.

It will also be noticed that the wind is never perfectly regular either in strength or direction, so that the waves in this kind of sea are seldom consistent; some are shorter than others and they cross each other's tracks. When the wind changes direction, the first wave system only decreases slowly and another system forms and combines with it. The different vintages meet and mingle with each other. The sea becomes chaotic and the waves don't hesitate to climb aboard.

Swell

Sometimes, in this type of chaotic sea, a slower, deeper rhythm can be felt coming from a direction that is quite different from that of the actual wind, apparently with a life of its own. On some calm days, the swell appears in great splendour: the sea is smooth and huge regular rollers undulate over its surface. They can be very high, but, above all, they are very long, with as much as two or three hundred metres between them. Waves have become swell by the time they leave the turbulent battlefield where the wind has stirred them into existence or, to speak more scientifically, when they leave their generating basin. Caused by a distant wind, far away in the North Atlantic for instance, which has since stopped or changed direction, these waves have gained considerable power, and they only diminish gradually. The shorter waves disappear first and a regular, harmonious movement is slowly established. The height of the waves gradually lessens while their length increases.

The swell created like this can roll for hundreds, even thousands of miles. The longer the waves are the further it will persist and it can sometimes be seen reaching the coast, when the weather is fine, the wind light or non-existent, and the sun blazing. It breaks white on the rocks along the shore – the sea is 'working'. You can be sure that somewhere, far out on the open sea, the wind has blown hard yesterday or two days ago. According to the height and frequency of the waves, you can even make an approximate calculation of the strength of the wind and how far away it was blowing.

This kind of swell is sometimes a forerunner of bad weather, for the waves themselves can travel faster than the wind that created them. The wind acts upon the liquid particles and their orbital movement is less than the velocity of the series of waves set in motion. A wind of 10 miles an hour can thus very easily supply enough power to waves to give them a velocity of 12 miles. This disparity becomes noticeable after a certain time, as the waves get well ahead of the wind. Very often therefore the swell precedes the disturbance which has created it and it is as well to be on the lookout in calm weather when the ground swell begins to make itself felt.

Wave obstructions

The state of the sea varies greatly as a result of any obstruction the waves encounter. One of the most spectacular changes takes place when waves (and the wind which drives them) clash with an opposing tidal stream. They are then braked, strangled as it were, between wind and current, their length is reduced, their height increased, their steepness can become excessive and they break. When wind is against tide you often therefore have a broken, very steep sea which can be dangerous. But, when wind and tide are in the same direction, the waves lengthen, become smoother and there is less likelihood of their breaking.

The nature of the sea bottom will also affect the waves. If the bottom rises abruptly, they are suddenly braked, as they are when they meet a contrary current and their height

increases and they break. These are the characteristic *breakers* of shoal water. The areas with strong tidal streams are often shallow (the races, for instance) and it is easily understood why memorable seas are encountered in them.

As they approach the coast, other phenomena can occur. When the rise in the sea bottom is not progressive but sudden, the waves will all for certain break in the same place, which is called a *bar*. On some coasts, this bar can be seen a long way off. On others it is very localised, forming at the mouth an estuary where an accumulation of sediment brought down by the river creates a shoal which the waves cannot cross without breaking.

Another factor is that the swell can change direction considerably when it approaches an island or a headland. Then the phenomenon of 'diffraction' can be seen (dramatically in aerial photographs) and it is analogous to those which affect sound and light waves. The swell passes on either side of the island and re-forms beyond it. The interference of the two lines of swell often brings about a confused sea for some distance. A swell can pass round a headland or a mere jetty, and often makes an anchorage dangerous which you had assumed to be safe.

Eventually all waves die away. When they reach shallow water, the movement of the water particles becomes elliptical, and flattens. Braked by the bottom, the waves slow down but increase in height. At the last moment, owing to friction, the bottom of the wave is retarded and the crest carries on, overspills and breaks.

As the depth of waves is related to their length, the longest waves – that is the oldest – touch the bottom very soon and can, as a result, increase enormously before reaching the shore. It is the longest and slowest swell which produces the strongest surf. It is a splendid sight to see waves rearing up in the air when the sun is dazzlingly bright, regaining their youthful vigour before they die in a myriad flashing lights. On coasts that shelve very gradually they can run on for a long time just on the point of breaking. It is then, that, balanced on a simple board, on the crest of a wave, you can experience for a few moments the unparalleled glory of surfing before crashing in a burst of foam on the hot sand.

Beaufort Scale Force Four-Five

3 The Weather

Now that the principal atmospheric phenomena have been concisely explained in the last chapter, it is time to see how they work for yachtsmen. We shall concentrate on the areas we know – the North Atlantic, the English Channel and the western Mediterranean. But these regions illustrate weather in general and Americans will know what allowances to make.

To speak of 'average weather' in any one area is to make even more unreliable statements than to describe the atmosphere in the same terms. You can sketch out the vast overall atmospheric movements without much risk of error, but establishing patterns for daily weather is a chancy business. So as not to lose our way, we shall keep closely, for the moment, to what can be observed. The approach of oceanic weather, in particular, can, it seems to us, be effectively foreseen by looking for characteristic skies. The identification of typical or significant skies may appear complicated as the sky is the most changeable landscape in the world, but it is worthwhile although all predictions must be qualified. Provided allowance is made for the unforeseen, the principal weather patterns that appear throughout the year can be interpreted, at least in the Atlantic areas. In the Mediterranean, the patterns are much less trustworthy. All kinds of local anomalies have to be taken into consideration and predictions are more speculative.

There is an amusing reference to 'knocking the skies into shape' in a well known song about 'Professor Nimbus' by Georges Brassens, the celebrated French poet and singer, but, thank God, we haven't yet reached the stage of controlling the weather. At the end of the chapter, when we go beyond present to future weather, it is principally to give the reader the basic elements of a field of research which is never finished.

Maritime weather

The north-west Atlantic region is a transit area where air masses meet, exchange places and pass through. The weather is in fact very varied. However, it is possible to sketch out a simple overall picture of it, even if it has to be modified later.

The weather there is influenced principally by the great centres of activity – the Azores anticyclone and the Icelandic depression. Their respective positions and strengths determine the latitude at which the polar and tropical air masses meet – i.e. the latitude of the polar front.

In winter, the anticyclone remains in low latitudes; it hardly ever comes further north than the 40th parallel. The Icelandic depression makes ground southwards and the polar front comes into our latitudes. The clash of these air masses creates disturbances that are carried along in the general west–east stream of the temperate regions and frequently reach the British Isles and France. We then speak of *unsettled westerly weather*.

Unsettled

In summer, the Azores anticyclone extends towards the north and the Icelandic depression remains in very high latitudes. The disturbances associated with the polar front are pushed beyond the 60th parallel and they move from Greenland to Scandinavia without reaching us. We are then in *anticyclonic conditions*.

Of course this pattern is susceptible to all kinds of variations and not only in spring and autumn. It isn't always fine in summer! The Azores anticyclone is usually very stable at its western edge but much less so at its eastern limit, where it breaks down periodically and creates disturbances. Some summers, for reasons not yet understood, the anticyclone does not come up as high as usual. We then speak of a 'wretched season' for the polar front is still with us.

In the same way, the winter season is not one long continuous westerly gale. The Siberian anticyclone sometimes extends to our regions and diverts the disturbance to the south or the north, bringing dry, cold weather.

All these very general data bring out one basic fact and its practical importance cannot escape anyone: the weather experienced on the Atlantic coasts and in the English Channel depends entirely on whether the disturbances of the polar front do or do not pass our way. These disturbances are a vital influence which is now our immediate concern.

Disturbances of the polar front

A mass of warm air originating in the tropics moves around the Azores anticyclone and makes its way towards the NE. A mass of cold air coming from the pole moves around the Icelandic depression and makes its way SW. These two masses of air meet somewhere off Newfoundland. The boundary between them is called a *frontal zone* and the line where it intersects the surface is called a *front*.

This frontal zone is not necessarily disturbed. When the two air masses are not moving at great speed, and their temperature and humidity are not very different, the convergence can be tranquil.

Sometimes the warm air mass pushes the cold air mass back to the north, but in doing so, as it is lighter than the cold air, it is forced to rise over it. The new frontal zone inclines therefore up towards the pole almost horizontal to the surface (the slope is about 1/100 to 1/1000) and results in what is called a *warm front*.

Sometimes it happens the other way round and it is the cold air mass that pushes the warm air mass before it. The heavier cold air undercuts the warm air, and forces it to rise,

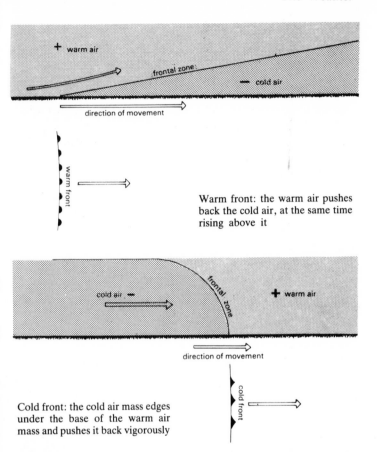

Warm front: the warm air pushes back the cold air, at the same time rising above it

Cold front: the cold air mass edges under the base of the warm air mass and pushes it back vigorously

forming a *cold front*. The frontal zone also slopes up towards the north, but it is much steeper than in the case of a warm front (in the order of 1/50).

When the temperature differences between the air masses are slight, the fronts are not very active, even weak as, for instance, when the flows of cold and warm air are moving parallel to one another or almost so. The polar front then takes on, alternatively, the characteristics of a warm front and a cold front, without any notable disturbances. The front is then said to be *stationary*.

But this kind of situation rarely lasts long. Most of the time the warm air masses and the cold air masses, which leave their places of origin for unpredictable reasons, travel at different speeds and with very distinctly different characteristics. Then they clash. The edge of the polar front becomes very clear cut, and it is then that there is, scientifically speaking, *frontogenesis*. The polar front, under pressure by the air masses, is distorted and develops undulations, each one of which can create a disturbance.

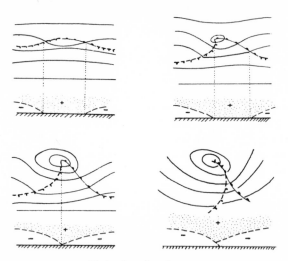

Birth of a disturbance

Clash of the air masses

The warm air mass making towards the NE tends to repulse the cold air mass coming from the opposite direction and at the same time rising above it. A wedge of warm air, in consequence, advances over the cold air; and its right-hand side forms an embryo warm front. The cold air, checked in its forward thrust, in turn makes an inroad with its left side into the warm air, and forms the beginnings of a cold front. The forward edges of the two air masses are then turned away from their original direction and an anti-clockwise movement begins, called *cyclogenesis*. A depression then forms at the extremity of the warm air and this eddy (or vortex), once it has taken shape, starts on a sort of life of its own. The whole of this phenomenon (the disturbance and the depression associated with it) then usually set off on an easterly course, towards Europe.

In its early life the disturbance consists, at ground level, of warm air advancing and replacing cold air (i.e. a *warm front*), a *warm sector* (the tip of the warm air itself) and of cold air, as it advances, replacing warm air (i.e. a *cold front*). The cold air surrounding the warm sector is sometimes referred to as the cold sector.

Once under way the disturbance gradually extends, covering hundreds sometimes even thousands of miles. All this time its depressionary characteristics are becoming accentuated and its structure is evolving. As the cold front moves more quickly than the warm front, it gradually catches up on the latter. The warm sector separating them is compressed and the warm air is slowly driven upwards by the thrust of the cold air behind the cold front. Finally the cold front catches up the warm front, and an *occlusion* occurs. This occlusion begins in the narrowest part of the warm sector and gradually extends over the whole of the front, until there is only one *occluded* front, which in turn is driven upwards. The characteristics of this front depend eventually on the temperature difference of the cold air ahead and behind it. If the air behind the occlusion is not so cold as the air which precedes it, it rises over the latter: this is an occlusion with warm front characteristics; but if the cold air behind the occlusion is the colder of the two, it penetrates below the preceding cold air and there is an occlusion with cold front characteristics.

From this moment on the disturbance begins to run down, the depression is closed up or occluded and the whole occluded front gradually weakens and finally disappears. This is *frontolysis*. The disturbance has now died, after having lasted only a few days, perhaps a week. The path it has followed has varied according to the shape of the field of pressure it has crossed. If an anticyclone was protecting the Atlantic, it would be diverted towards the north to die away on the coast of Scandinavia. Had the anticyclone been situated over the British Isles, it might have been diverted towards the south and lost itself in the Mediterranean.

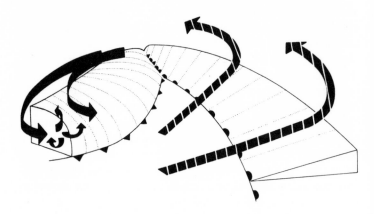

Movements of air masses in a disturbance

But all is not over yet. We have already seen that when the polar front was distorted under the thrust of the air masses, several wave movements were formed and each one of them gave rise to a disturbance. The first disturbance is therefore followed by all the rest of the group. This *family of disturbances* numbers on average four to six members advancing in order of age: the eldest go in front, more or less occluded, followed by the younger ones which still have some impetus and often travel further south than older ones.

Eventually, after the last disturbance has gone, the polar air arrives for the final grand 'sweep up'. As this is rarely uniform, we can still suffer some *cold secondary fronts*, which often have violent effects. But peace returns at last. The invasion of cold air brings with it a general rise in the pressure and finally what the average tourist calls 'fine weather' and meteorologists, in their more guarded language, call simply *an interval*.

Passage of a disturbance

This description of the birth and development of a family of disturbance is obviously rudimentary and rather theoretical. In reality each disturbance, like every living creature, has its own character, formed by the nature of the confrontation that originated it; it is also changed throughout the whole of its existence under all sorts of influences. A disturbance can take on all kinds of shapes. Once it is launched on the highways of the sky, it does not necessarily follow a straight and predictable path. Disturbances can be seen to speed up or slow down suddenly, or even stop for a while. Some change direction, split in two or interfere with other disturbances that have originated elsewhere. The depression accompanying them can deepen suddenly and quite unpredictably, or

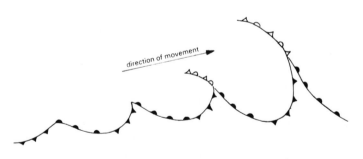

A family of disturbances

fill earlier than can be foreseen. With such individual 'meteorological types' anything can be expected.

Such differences must not however be allowed to obscure the fundamental similarity in the basic structure of each.

Generally speaking the passage of a disturbance over the area where one is sailing is marked by a series of phenomena which follow each other in an order, which reveals precise organisation. These phenomena come about essentially through marked variations in temperature, pressure, wind and the look of the sky.

Temperature. People have to bear alternately the consequences of the passage of cold polar air, warm tropical air and then cold air again. The variations cause chills and the pharmaceutical industry reaps the harvest.

Pressure and wind. The pressure variations are clearly illustrated in the diagram below. When the warm air mass makes progress, pressure drops. It is at its lowest when the warm air mass has invaded the whole of the sky; that is the moment the warm front and the warm sector are passing by. It rises rapidly thereafter with the arrival of denser cold air.

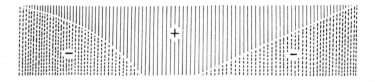

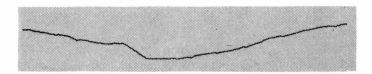

As a warm front approaches, the dense cold air is gradually replaced by warm, lighter air: the barometer falls. On the arrival of the cold front, the warm air is in its turn replaced by cold air: the barometer rises

We know too that, around a depression, the wind turns in an anti-clockwise direction and that it strengthens as the depression deepens. Anyone on the line of the depression's advance can observe (and the weather map will confirm) that

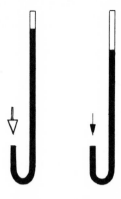

Torricelli's experiment: the mercury in the tube rises more or less according to the weight of the air outside. Cold air: high pressures. Warm air: low pressures

the wind comes first from the SE or south, veers gradually to SW and from there to NW at the end of the depression. A subsequent examination of the map gives an accurate appreciation of what has been observed on the ground: the direction of the wind quite clearly changes with the passage of the warm front (shown cutting across the isobars), stays in the same quarter while the warm sector moves across (shown by the straight isobars) and veers again with the passage of the cold front. The spacing of the isobars allows an estimate to be made of wind strength at any given point in the depression. It is usually observed that the strongest winds are in the southern part of the depression, at some distance from the centre (50 to 200 miles) and immediately after the cold front passes on.

These variations of wind strength and direction produce big changes in the state of the sea. The strength of the wind increases the size of the waves, but its rotation in particular sets up differing wave systems, the first coming from the south or SW, the last from NW or north. The interference patterns of these wave systems often stirs up a lumpy sea both on the arrival of the cold front and during the invasion of polar air that follows it. When several disturbances follow each other, we are finally left with many wave systems which clash with each other, producing a confused sea.

The Weather

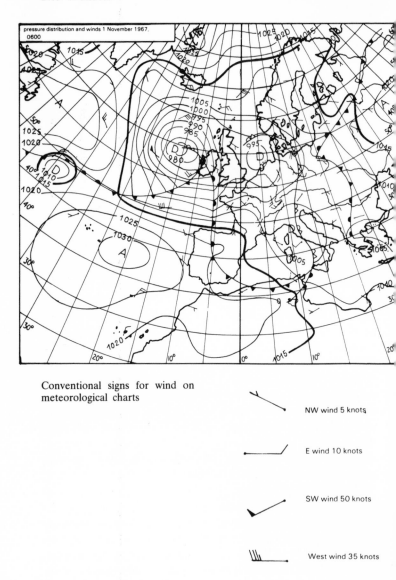

pressure distribution and winds 1 November 1967.
0600

Conventional signs for wind on
meteorological charts

NW wind 5 knots

E wind 10 knots

SW wind 50 knots

West wind 35 knots

The appearance of the sky. As you would suspect, the great confusion to which the air masses are being subjected encourages the growth of significant cloud formations, but there is a new factor: these cloud formations do not wander at will across the sky, but, on the contrary, their distribution in space and sequence in time are so distinctive that they constitute a *cloud system*, an ordered grouping, covering several different areas giving the whole sky classic characteristics.

There are cloud sequences, as we shall see. The one accompanying a disturbance of the polar front (known in full as 'moving extra-tropical depressionary cloud sequence') is the most characteristic of all. Each of these zones corresponds to an exact moment of the disturbance and gives it its name. An observer stationed in the line of advance of the disturbance will see, passing in succession, the *head* (the area in front of the depression), the *body* (the area at the centre of the depression), the warm sector and the *wake* (the area behind the depression). An observer situated a little further north will only see the *cold edge*; situated a little further south he will only pick out the *warm edge* and eventually the *boundary zone* which links this disturbance to the one that follows it.

The disclosing of such a cloud sequence is particularly valuable for us. Knowing the different faces of the sky makes it possible to see that a disturbance is on its way, to assess one's position in relation to it, and to follow the different stages of its development. We shall therefore base our detailed analysis on the description of the principal *patterns of sky* that characterise this development.

The sky during a depression

It is already clear that any definition of a sky type must not be taken too literally. The cloud sequences vary greatly from one depression to another, according to their age and the time of year. The really typical sequences only occur, for the most part, in winter. In summer, the time which most interests us, we have to deal usually with *weakened* sequences which have rather different characteristics. There are all sorts of variants to take into account, even if that makes for complications.

Head

The head of the cloud sequence is characterised by a sky of well ordered cirrus, progressively invading the sky, accompanied by a thin veil of cirrostratus or altostratus. The pressure drops slowly. The wind tends to back southerly and freshen.

The head of the system corresponds to the arrival of warm, damp air at altitude. It begins a long way from the central part of the disturbance – usually several hundreds of miles.

The warm air rises slowly above the cold air and expands; when it has reached a height of six or seven kilometres, its water vapour is changed into ice crystals. The first clouds to appear are therefore cirrus, of the type *uncinus* (in the shape of commas or hooks), or *fibratus* (of fibrous appearance). They are also called 'messengers' since they announce the approach of a disturbance. They come from a well determined quarter of the horizon (usually west or SW), where they appear very dense.

The sky remains clear and fine weather cumulus can still be seen. However, it will be seen to flatten and this flattening is due to a lessening of the convection, limited by the warm air high up.

The light is often very clear during these first hours and visibility is very good. 'Too good', say the coastal observers who have noticed this abnormal visibility the day before and have deduced an imminent change in the weather.

The light grows gradually dimmer. Following the cirrus and coming from the same direction, cirrostratus drifts in and soon covers the whole sky, bringing with it those halos that form round the sun and moon. In reality the appearance of cirrus and cirrostratus does not mean with absolute certainty that you are in the head of a disturbance. They appear too, as we shall see, on the cold edge where everything clears

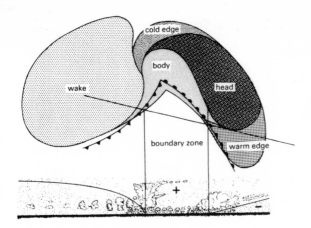

Cloud system in a young disturbance

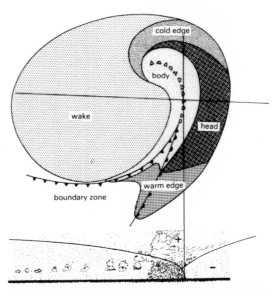

Cloud system in an occluded disturbance

Head sky

up quickly. The fact that the barometer begins to drop and that the wind backs SE is not conclusive either. But the sky's ceiling begins to lower slowly. The warm air mass makes further progress and after the cirrostratus we soon have altostratus, a middle layer cloud, covering the sky. This altostratus is still quite thin, it is the *translucidus* type, first slightly bluish, then changing to grey. This cloud intimates the end of the head and the beginning of the body of the disturbance.

In summer, when we are in a weakened system, the head sky is not necessarily characteristic: the cirrus are less regularly organised and are rarely followed by cirrostratus. It even happens that no cirrus is observed and that the only clouds composing the head are altocumulus. These are laid out like an enormous pavement through which the blue of the sky can still be made out (altocumulus stratiformis perlucidus) or they take on a cylindrical or boulder-like form (undulatus) or even suggest cuttle fish bones (lenticularis).

Here too the expert can be mistaken and think that he is on the warm edge of the system, which is characterised by the presence of extensive, numerous altocumulus.

Body

The body of the sequence is characterised by the appearance of a continuous layer of altostratus or nimbostratus, frequently coupled with low ragged clouds, and it all generally leads to steady rain. The pressure drops still further and reaches its lowest point with the arrival of the warm front. The wind that has gone on strengthening veers from the south to SW or to west.

The warm air mass now spreads into the lower layers of the sky. The altostratus translucidus is followed by thicker and thicker altostratus opacus and the clouds drop lower and lower. It may have already begun to rain. Usually visibility is still quite good, right up to the moment when the 'rack' appears – small black clouds scudding under the grey vault, cumulus fractus foreshadowing heavy rain. These little clouds precede the arrival of the enormous nimbostratus. It rains then without stopping, often for hours. Visibility becomes poor and even plain bad as the lowest part of the nimbostratus passes over, with the arrival of the warm front.

Body sky

At this stage the warm air mass occupies all the sky, the thermometer rises, the barometer is at its lowest point and the wind veers quite noticeably (between 20 to 40°) to SW or west.

The newly arrived warm air is usually stable, but it can be unstable, and cumulus convectus or cumulonimbus can develop above the altostratus or the nimbostratus. They are not seen but their presence is disclosed by more irregular rain, sometimes thunder with violent squalls.

In a weakened system, the nimbostratus can be absent, and the altostratus itself has a structure like that of altocumulus, accompanied sometimes by ragged clouds and giving lighter and intermittent rain.

At this stage of the description distinctions must be made between new and old disturbances. In the case of a newly formed disturbance, a warm sector succeeds the warm front. After this we are in the 'second part' of the body associated with the passage of the cold front. This is the case we are going to study here. When we are in the middle of a more developed disturbance, the cold front follows hard upon the warm front, without the intermediary sector being noticed. Occluded disturbances are different again and will be examined towards the end of this chapter.

Warm sector

In a warm sector, the sky is generally very low and covered by an often continuous layer of stratocumulus, sometimes accompanied by fog. There is a light drizzle. Barometric pressure and wind remain almost constant until the arrival of the cold front.

The warm air mass from now on occupies the whole sky. Normally, during the passage of a warm sector, the rain stops, the ceiling tends to rise a bit and is composed of fairly compact stratocumulus and there may be drizzle near hills and coasts. The appearance of this type of cloud is connected with the turbulence caused by the friction of the air at sea level.

Warm sector sky

A little to the south of the disturbance, in the zone which links it to the next disturbance, known as the boundary zone, visibility is sometimes bad, with stratus low overhead, at least during winter.

In summer, the warm sector and the boundary zone are usually not so cloudy.

As the cold front approaches, the sky may become dark again or, in winter, the overcast is strengthened. This is where the body of the disturbance is found.

The cold front itself is made up of a quite formidable sort of barrier. The cold posterior air is pushing back violently on the rear of the warm air mass. This warm air is then driven suddenly upwards and becomes unstable. Cumulus congestus and cumulonimbus, often huge, loom up and create a *line squall* along which blow fierce gusts of wind and there are violent showers, sometimes thunderstorms. When this cold front arrives, the wind frequently backs briefly to SW, then veers sharply NW and suddenly there is sunshine again; but it is colder.

Wake

This last part of the disturbance is characterised by a variable sky, with alternating bright periods and cloudy stretches producing showers, squalls or thunderstorms. The barometer begins to rise rapidly. The wind settles in the NW and often freshens again.

The sky in the wake is one of the loveliest. Cold air then reigns supreme and, as soon as it appears, the thermometer falls considerably while the barometer rises. This cold air, warmed through its base being in contact with the sea, becomes unstable. As a result, the wake sky has burgeoning clouds, cumulonimbus generating violent squalls, and cumulus congestus with strong vertical development, sometimes producing showers and almost always strengthening wind. In the bright periods, visibility is excellent. The sky is an intense blue or sometimes takes on the pale green tint peculiar to polar air. The wind is often very strong and, above all, irregular. For yachtsmen the wake is often the most dangerous part of the disturbance.

In summer, this wake does not always have its classic

Wake sky

characteristics. The cumulonimbus are often absent, and there is always cumulus and the somewhat menacing cumulus congestus. They are sometimes accompanied by altostratus and banks of stratocumulus.

The wake of a disturbance can be very broad. It can extend over a thousand kilometres or more and its passage can last for over twenty-four hours. Very often, in a wake sky, the first cirrus of the following disturbance begin to appear. When there is no other disturbance to come, the weather gradually calms down, the wind veers north and the big clouds disappear. Soon all that is left in the sky are a few cumulus *humilis* – by far the best type of cumulus.

Cold edge

An observer situated a little to the north of a disturbance's line of advance sees the passage of cold edge of the sequence. He remains in the polar air and does not experience the passage of any front. In reality, disturbances usually circulate too far north for cold edge skies to be seen at all frequently in our latitudes. It can nevertheless happen, especially in winter, and it is worth knowing their characteristics for they can easily be mistaken for a head sky. In fact the cold edge of this cloud sequence is characterised by a veil of cirrostratus, either partial or complete, sometimes following cirrus. Pressure drops and the wind turns SE. It is only too easy to be misled.

However, this veil of cirrostratus, instead of thickening, gradually disperses and soon other clouds belonging to other types of sky begin to appear. Pressure rises and the wind, instead of veering south, backs through east gradually to north.

Warm edge

Much more frequently one is situated a little to the south of a disturbance, on the track of the warm edge and the boundary zone which follows it.

The warm edge sky is characterised by isolated banks of

Cold edge sky ▲

▼ Warm edge sky

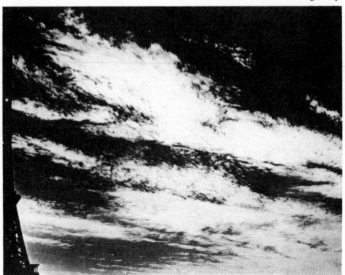

altocumulus, spread in an irregular pattern, not very extensive, often lenticular in shape and in a state of change. These
clouds are preceded generally by cirrus and sometimes
accompanied by cirrocumulus.

The frequent presence of altocumulus lenticularis, of cirrocumulus (early in the morning) and especially the contin-
uously changing sky are the clearest proofs that you are in
this warm edge, where variations of pressure and wind are
otherwise very slow.

The sky is never completely covered. The cloudiness of
the altocumulus, once it attains its maximum, decreases. On
land and principally in summer, a sky associated with a ridge
of high pressure (which we shall examine later) often returns
then and the effects of the disturbance are not felt. On the
sea, banks of stratus and stratocumulus may appear and you
then have an overcast sky which is associated with a boundary zone and the disturbance that follows.

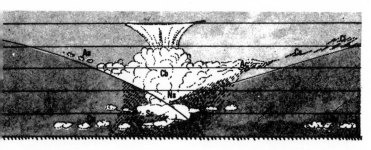

An occluded front is often characterised by dense cloud cover

Occluded front

The arrival of an occluded disturbance is heralded by a quite
normal head sky. But the body of the disturbance has particular characteristics as it is only made up of one front, the
cold front having caught up with the warm one. The occluded front usually looks at first almost like a warm front, but
the line of cumulonimbus of the old cold front follows

Beaufort Scale Force Seven-Eight

immediately, or even appears to be fused with the nimbostratus (or the altostratus if the warm air mass has already
been driven to some height).

In fact, the bases of all these clouds are very much alike.
But precipitation changes the pattern, showers succeeding
continuous rain; the veer of the wind is considerable, the
barometer rises rapidly and the temperature drops. All these
signs indicate that we are dealing with an occluded front. It
will also be noticed that this occluded front is often remarkable for the amount of cloud present (much stratocumulus,
stratus fractus or cumulus fractus) and partial superimposi-
tion of the different cloud layers often brings on heavy rain.

84

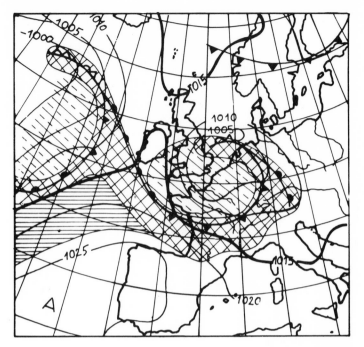

wake

body

boundary
zone

Fine weather skies

The term fine weather is ambiguous, and normally meteorologists are careful not to use it. Yet fine weather exists, as we
know by experience, and it would be a shame to camouflage
it under a scientific name which would, to coin a metaphor,
cast a shadow on it. All that is required is to agree about
what the term means.

For a sailor, fine weather isn't necessarily sunny weather,
nor should it be too calm for we need wind to sail. What we
want most is well established, clear weather that we can rely
on. In meteorological terms, this is weather associated with a
passing ridge of high pressure, characterised by the absence

of disturbance on the polar front or stormy formations. The sky patterns associated with this weather are outside all organised cloud sequences. Three principal skies of this type can be recognised: the one associated with a ridge of high pressure, a stratiform sky and the sky of instability.

Sky associated with a ridge of high pressure
This is a clear sky, or with some cumulus not greatly developed vertically, and sometimes a few isolated banks of cloud in the middle and upper layers.

This type can be seen in all latitudes and at all times of the year. But it is in particular the classical fine-weather summer sky. Its appearance means that we are in a unified, stable mass of air, sometimes without enough moisture for clouds to form.

This kind of sky is called 'clear or partly cloudy' when the amount of cloud is nil or below 3 octas.* It is 'cloudy or partly cloudy' when the amount of cloud is for a time between 3 and 8 octas. These two categories of sky can alternate in the course of a single day; the cumulus composing it usually develops considerably over the coast during the day. Over the sea, convection occurs mainly at night. If the convection stops the cumulus always decrease, and then disappear.

In addition to the cumulus, the following can also be encountered in a sky associated with a ridge of high pressure:

– stratus, sometimes masking the upper sky, particularly over the land and in estuaries;
– isolated banks of stratocumulus or even altocumulus, especially in the evening, because these clouds result from the development of the cumulus by day;
– dense cirrus (spissatus), but in no organised fashion.

---

*Meteorologists evaluate cloud cover in eighths or 'octas': 8 octas means the sky is completely covered.

This weather is also often characterised by:

- slight mists which hardly hamper visibility but give the sky the 'washed blue' colour, typical of fine anticyclonic weather;
- advection fogs which can cover all the English Channel, for instance, in spring and in NE winds;
- the appearance of dew even before the sun has set: towards the end of the afternoon the deck is often wet (with fresh water), and it remains wet all night and only dries in the sun next morning.

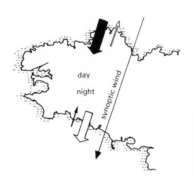

In a NE synoptic wind: offshore wind strong in South Brittany at night, slight in North Brittany; sea breeze slight in South Brittany by day, strong in North Brittany

Land and sea breezes

This type of sky, with little cloud, is characteristic of a shallow pressure gradient. It encourages land and sea breezes, which happily take over from an often weak synoptic wind (the synoptic wind being the normal wind connected with the pressure gradient).

We have analysed the principle behind these breezes in the preceding chapter: a sea breeze blows during the day and is 'drawn in' by the rising air over the heated land; a land breeze blows at night when the land has cooled and the sea is now warmer than it is. The strength of these breezes is therefore bound up during the day with the strength of the sunlight and the cooling of the earth by radiation at night.

This 'play' of land and sea breezes happens at various points along the coast, but the conditions in which it becomes established vary from one place to another. These breezes are not always alternating, and they follow, to some extent, the movement of the sun (this is why they are often called *solar breezes*): a NE breeze in the morning, turning east then SE and dying away usually before midday, to pick up again from the SW in the afternoon and to come round to NW or north in the evening. It disappears again and picks up from the NE in the latter half of the night.

When the synoptic wind is weak or non-existent, these breezes predominate. When it has some strength, they may well combine with it, modifying its direction, either reinforcing or reducing it. Here are some typical consequences of a NE synoptic wind: in south Brittany, a fresh or even very fresh NE wind at night and a weak NE wind, calm, or a weak SW breeze during the day; in north Brittany on the other hand, a fresh NE wind by day, and a weak NE wind, calm or a SW breeze at night.

The distance to which the breezes are felt at sea is very variable. It usually extends about 5 or 10 miles offshore, and sometimes, but very rarely, up to 20 miles.

Turbulent sky

A **stratiform** or turbulent sky is composed of stratocumulus in a continuous layer, and sometimes stratus. There is normally no precipitation or, if there is any, very weak (in the form of drizzle, granular snow or ice needles).

This definition is enough for we are dealing now essentially with fine winter weather, those peaceful grey days when a great cloak of stratocumulus stratiformis, capable sometimes of covering the whole of Europe, spreads far and wide.

This type of sky (known as anticyclonic gloom) can, however, be met with at all times of the year and in any latitude, in areas of high pressure or at their edges.

On land, it is usually the result of the turbulence caused by the friction of the air over the Earth's surface. Stratocumulus which cover the sky can last for several days consecutively in the same area. Temporary lifting of the cloud layer can occur at the warmest times of day.

This type of sky is rare in summer, but then it discloses a very clear daytime development: the stratocumulus form during the night and are reabsorbed quite quickly in the course of the morning.

At sea, a stratus sky often forms in the lower layers of warm damp air that arrive over colder waters (the New-foundland fogs). This type of sky often marks the boundary zone of a series of disturbances.

It is to be remembered that a stratiform sky, usually very low, may be hiding another sky type that is developing above it.

Sky of instability

A cumuliform sky is composed of cumulus congestus which can develop into cumulonimbus and be accompanied by showers and sometimes thunderstorms.

Unstable sky

This type of sky indicates fairly strong vertical instability in the heart of a large air mass. It is very much like the wake sky (the area behind a depression), but it is always outside any organised cloud system.

It is uncommon in northern latitudes, where great masses of warm, damp unstable air do not often occur. But it can come across in the Mediterranean at night, for instance. It arises then from a very marked development of a sky associated with a ridge of high pressure: the cumulus reach and pass the stage of cumulus congestus to become cumulonimbus, causing storms at night, although during the day the weather is calm and the sky clear. On land, it happens in reverse: the development takes place during the day and the storms break towards the end of the afternoon.

An alternation of unstable skies and skies associated with a ridge of high pressure can be observed several days running without the least change in the air mass or the approach of a cloud sequence.

Thunder storm skies

The concept of thundery weather is not necessarily any easier to define than fine weather. Apart from the more spectacular features, we may be dealing with unsettled weather, strangely 'disordered' without any clear-cut characteristics. You can't always be sure about it.

Two kinds of thundery weather of different origins can be observed. The first is the result of the development of a sky of relatively fine weather, when the convection, at night at sea, by day on land, is sufficiently strong to change inoffensive cumulus into cumulus congestus or cumulonimbus. This type of thunder storm is born in a unified mass of air, which, having been heated strongly from below, has become unstable. In our latitudes, this development only happens during summer and usually in barometric 'fens'.

It is in its turn clearly influenced by local conditions: the nature of the land and sea surface, hills and undulations, wind and any other factor that influences the temperature

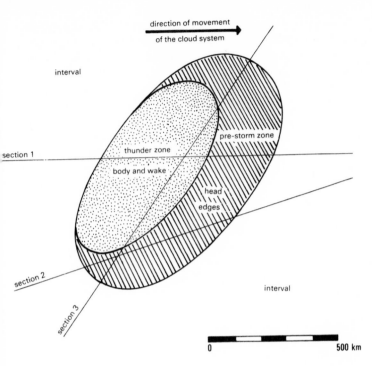

Thunder storm cloud system

and humidity of the lower layers of the atmosphere.

The other type of thunder storm appears in polar front disturbances. We have already spoken of them in describing the warm and cold fronts of such disturbances. Here the storms do not result from local conditions, but solely from the confrontation of air masses and their violence varies according to the degree of instability and humidity of the warm air mass.

Originating through the phenomenon of convection or linked to frontal instability, the thunder storms give rise to sufficiently characteristic cloud formations to be described as distinct cloud sequences. It is quite impossible to analyse the structure of these sequences as precisely as the cloud

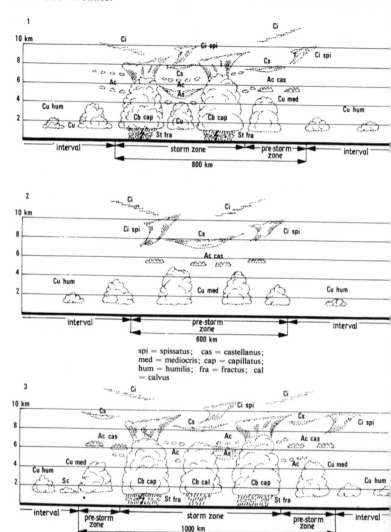

spi = spissatus;   cas = castellanus;
med = mediocris;   cap = capillatus;
hum = humilis;   fra = fractus;   cal
= calvus

Clouds in a thunder storm cloud system

sequences of depressions, but we can at least distinguish two kinds of sky: the *pre-thunder storm sky (head sky and edge sky) and the stormy sky (body sky and wake sky).*

Pre-thunder storm sky

This sky is characterised by dense cirrus and a thick partial veil of cirrostratus, accompanied with banks of altocumulus and occasionally cumulus.

These clouds, moving slowly, are in the van and on the edge of the storm system proper, and are at one and the same time, its head and its edges. The altocumulus castellanus or floccus appear as long as five or six hours before the storms; they are generally preceded or accompanied by quite dense cirrus, very varied in form: cirrus uncinus or spissatus in the shape of frothy flakes, fern leaves, vertebrae, tufts and suchlike. These cirrus are often the residue, brought by the wind, of old cumulonimbus anvils. Sheets of thick cirro-

Pre-thunder storm sky

Thunder storm sky

stratus may also appear and, lower down, stratocumulus or cumulus whose development in daytime is conspicuous.

This sky persists and extends as long as the general conditions, in particular the temperature and humidity in the lower layers, do not vary. It can happen that the storm does not break, but usually it is not far off.

Thunder clouds
This is a sky characterised by an overcast, chaotic, heavy, motionless appearance, with cloud elements of many different forms at all heights. It is usually accompanied by precipitation in the form of showers.

Thunder clouds normally follow the pre-thunder clouds but it can also result, and especially in summer, from:

- the change taking place in the body and wake of a depressionary cloud sequence that arrives in an area where the barometric gradient is slight;
- from the rapid development of cumulus congestus to the stage of cumulonimbus when, in areas where the convection was already very strong, conditions of instability occur in the middle and upper layers of the sky.

The stormy sky is characterised by the presence of convection clouds with much vertical development. In particular the budding of the upper part of these clouds, developing with startling rapidity, is noticeable. Cumulus congestus develop in all directions and change rapidly into formidable cumulonimbus. The latter, after a limited journey (usually less than 100 miles) during which they create squalls and violent gusts of wind, gradually disintegrate, leaving cloud banks or veils in the sky at different levels: cirrus and cirrostratus, altocumulus and stratocumulus of the most diverse shapes. Other cumulonimbus form in their turn, then disintegrate a little later, and the cycle begins again.

This disintegration of the cumulonimbus is the reason why one can see, in a thundery sky, such a great diversity of clouds at all levels. It is also for this reason that it is impossible to differentiate with any precision between the body sky and the wake sky.

In the relatively clear periods separating the storm centres, one often sees altocumulus castellanus or floccus. Layers of stratocumulus opacus or undulatus appear nearer the storm centres.

The extraordinary spectacle offered by a thundery sky can last for a few hours or several days. Sometimes, too, just when you think it is all over it begins again, with renewed fury.

Types of weather

The concept of weather types may seem unsatisfactory. In practice two exactly similar meteorological situations are seldom identical. However, analyses carried out over many years have established certain constants, certain 'models' of weather that occur sufficiently regularly and last long enough to give us reasonable hope that we shall encounter them again. A type of weather is a type of atmospheric circulation, linked generally to a particular season when it reappears frequently and persists for several days, even for several weeks.

This question of duration is important: when we speak of 'squally weather', for instance, or 'thick weather', we must realise that we are not dealing with a type of weather, but only with a particular phase of a much more general type of weather.

The prototypes of weather are based essentially on a study of the characteristic distribution of pressure on the Earth's surface and its day-to-day development. When weather begins to resemble one of these types, reproducing the overall conditions and developing in the same way, then we can accept that we are experiencing recognised patterns of weather.

It must be realised, however, that surface conditions may not be associated with the corresponding pressure fields at altitude. To recognise a weather pattern with certainty, we ought to consider at the same time the surface maps, and the upper air maps of the average atmosphere (in this context the surface is at 500m). This comparison can be made only by the professional meteorologist. We shall only deal here with the surface map, which allows a good enough analysis of the situation to be made, and we shall restrict ourselves to describing the most common types of weather encountered in the eastern Atlantic.

Disturbed patterns
Disturbed westerly airstream in high latitudes
A quite frequent situation in summer. The disturbances circulate up to the latitudes of the British Isles. The 1015 isobar (line of average pressure) passes to the north of the English Channel. The pressure is rather high in the Channel and in the Bay of Biscay.

The weather is only slightly disturbed over Brittany and in the Channel. Rain slight or nil. Fine clear periods and rapid improvement.

Wind mainly from the west, quite regular, Force 3 to 5, with some squalls as disturbances pass by.

Sea rough in the Channel, moderate swell.

Skies varied: alternating between sky associated with a ridge of high pressure, warm edge, boundary zone, sometimes wake.

Visibility generally good, reduced by mist on the edges, and by stratus in the boundary zones.

Outlook. This situation can develop as:

– *unfavourable*, if the Azores anticyclone weakens: the press-ure drops, and formidable secondary depressions can then circulate round the main centres of low pressure;

– *favourable*, if the anticyclone extends: the 1020 isobar coming a little higher in latitude, we then find ourselves in skies associated with ridges of high pressure and the winds are moderate.

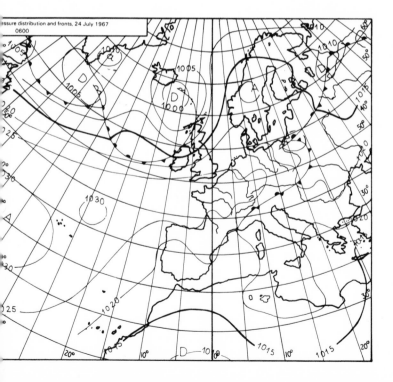

Pressure distribution and fronts, 24 July 1967 0600

97

The Weather

Disturbed westerly airstream in middle latitudes
A common situation at all times of year.

The disturbances cross France.

The 1015 isobar is situated almost on the 45th parallel. The pressure is below average in the Channel and in the Bay of Biscay.

Classic disturbed weather. The disturbances follow each other every 36 or 48 hours bringing heavy rain as the fronts pass through. Some of these disturbances can be very active, even in summer. The weather changes quickly.

Wind veers from SW to NW as the disturbances pass through; Force 4 to 6 generally, with increases on the arrival of the fronts.

Sea heavy for a short time, with broken swell.

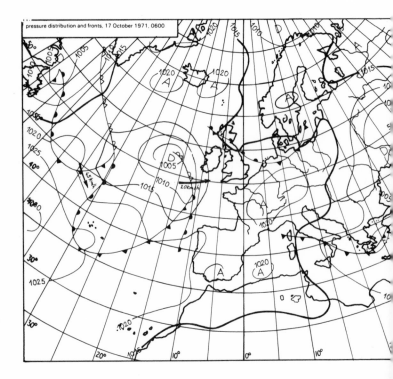

pressure distribution and fronts, 17 October 1971, 0600

Skies head, body, warm sector, wake, the cirrus of the following disturbance often appearing in the wake sky.
Visibility moderate in the body and warm sector skies.
Outlook. This situation can develop as:

– *Unfavourable*, if the disturbances which follow one another become deeper and deeper, with fronts and wakes more and more unmistakable;
– *Favourable*, when all the group of disturbances has passed: we have the grand 'clean up' of the north-westerly wind and the appearance of a wake sky more vigorous than the others, bringing an improvement and contributing to the formation of a ridge of high pressure (anticyclonic) over the east Atlantic.

Disturbed westerly airstream in low latitudes

A very frequent situation at the end of winter, rare in summer.

A depression is centred to the NW of the British Isles; a vast area of low pressure extends over the whole of Europe and the Mediterranean. The 1015 isobar is pushed to the south of Spain, pressure is particularly low and suffers only minor variations as the disturbances pass through. The pressure gradient still remains quite steep.

The weather is very disturbed, with long periods of rain and heavy weather on the open sea. The temperature is higher than normal for winter.

Wind mainly from the westerly sector, with the usual veering as the disturbances pass through; Force 4 to 6, reaching 7 and even more for short periods.
Sea heavy, sometimes very heavy, with westerly swell in all coastal areas.
Skies, the classic skies of depressionary systems, with vigorous wakes.
Visibility very variable, sometimes nil in the warm sectors, very good in the wakes.
Outlook. This situation can develop as:

– *Unfavourable*, if the 1015 isobar moves into a higher latitude: the pressure gradient increases, and violent winds occur;

– *Favourable*, if the depression fills: the gradient lessens, the wind abates. But the swell still persists for a long time.

Disturbed north-westerly airstream

A frequent situation in summer, especially during July. The Azores anticyclone extends off the Bay of Biscay, a stream of disturbances circulates to the north of the anticyclone. The 1015 isobar runs through the British Isles. Pressure is relatively high and varies little with the passage of the disturbances.

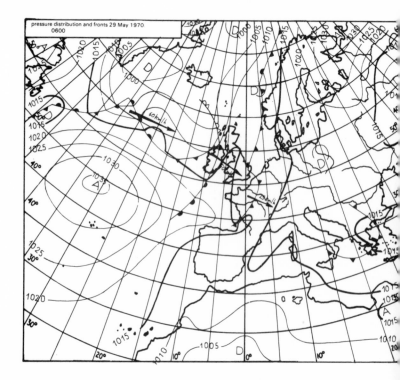

pressure distribution and fronts 29 May 1970 0600

Fine weather at sea, cooler than normal on the coasts, with frequent showers, especially in the Channel.

Wind mainly NW, very gusty. Turbulence and squalls.

Sea smooth with moderate swell from the NW.

Skies, warm edge, body and above all wake, the cold fronts or occlusions with cold front characteristics being dominant in this type of disturbance. Ridge-of-high-pressure skies between disturbances.

Visibility mainly good, less in squalls and showers. Fog rare.

Outlook. This situation can develop as:

– *Unfavourable* if the ridge that extends towards the Alps breaks down, allowing the disturbances to drop to lower latitudes (an infrequent occurrence); but if the gradient increases between the anticyclone and the depressionary area, we may expect strong winds from the NW to N in the Channel and over Brittany (a frequent occurrence);

– *Favourable*, if the anticyclone moves into higher latitudes: the disturbances are then pushed back towards the Baltic. The NW wind becomes moderate, under ridge-of-high-pressure skies.

Unsettled south-westerly weather

A very frequent situation in winter (from November to March); very rare in summer.

A depression is centred between Iceland and Scotland, a vast area of low pressure extending as far as Brittany and Normandy.

The 1015 isobar passes over the Vendée and curves up towards Denmark. Pressure remains average over Brittany and Normandy, but the gradient is steep.

A strong SW airstream passes over the east Atlantic, bringing warmer weather than normal (for instance 18° at Brest in February), but also drizzle and heavy, continuous rain. Heavy squalls of SW wind at sea.

Wind mainly SW, pouring into the Channel area.

High sea with heavy SW swell off Ireland, strong SW swell in the Channel.

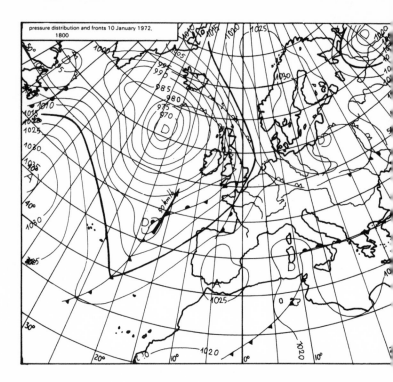

Skies, head, body, and above all strong warm sectors. The wakes are not very marked.

Visibility often below one mile in nimbostratus, stratus or fog.

Outlook. This situation can develop as:

– *Unfavourable*, if the pressure gradient increases: squalls of wind are to be expected; but, if small secondary depressions develop and circulate to the area of the Channel, local violent, brief storms can develop;
– *Favourable*, if the SW airstream shifts north; the wind abates and can even become very weak. This is 'the calm after the storm'.

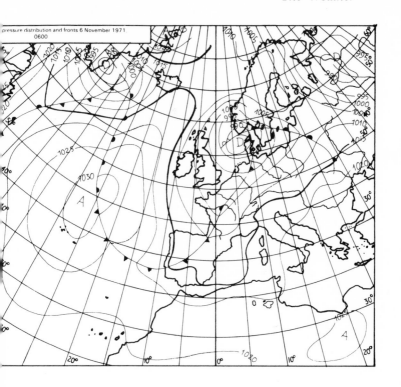

pressure distribution and fronts 6 November 1971
0600

Disturbed westerly airstream with trough

A quite common occurrence in spring, repeated at the end of summer and becoming very frequent in autumn.

In a westerly airstream, a fairly deep trough of low pressure crosses France.

The 1015 isobar is bent steeply south, pressure is very variable, without the gradient becoming steep.

The weather can be bad for short periods, with showers and stormy squalls. It develops quite slowly (average length of a depression is three days).

Wind turning from SSW to NNW and freshening as the disturbances move through; moderate between them.

Sea not at all rough usually, with SW or NW swells, rarely broken.

Skies, head, body and wake. The wakes can develop stormy characteristics, if the pressure gradient decreases appreciably; then pre-storm or even storm skies may appear.

Visibility limited under the cumulostratus, without the weather being really thick.

Outlook. This situation can develop as:

– *Unfavourable*, if it takes a stormy turn, or if a direct polar air stream comes and reactivates a current disturbance;
– *Favourable*, if the Azores anticyclone moves north, the weather improves.

Disturbed airstream in a col

A very frequent situation towards the end of spring and at the beginning of summer.

An area of relatively low pressures joining two depressions stretches from west to east at the latitude of the British Isles.

The 1015 isobar passes on either side of this line. Pressure is below average to the west of Brittany and in the Channel, but it is not subject to much variation.

Small moving depressions run from west to east in the col, giving rain for short periods. Weather colder than normal to the north of the col is noted; weather warmer than normal, quite dry and with little cloud to the south.

Wind well established in the western sector veering as the disturbances pass through, usually without any noteworthy increases in strength.

Sea moderate to rough with westerly swell.

Skies, ridge-of-high-pressure or boundary zone.

Visibility reduced for a time in boundary zones and as warm fronts move through.

Outlook. This situation can develop as:

– *Unfavourable*, if the pressure gradient increases and the

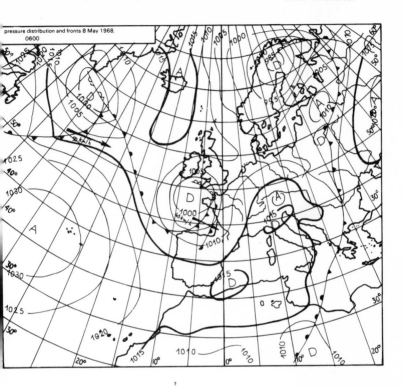

pressure distribution and fronts 8 May 1968. 0600

depressions moving through deepen;

– *Favourable*, if an anticyclonic ridge settles in place of the col and drives the stream of disturbances north. But this ridge is often fragile; a head sky appearing in its western part heralds another worsening in the weather.

Anticyclonic patterns

High pressures in the west of Europe

A frequent situation in May, June and sometimes July.

An anticyclone is centred over the British Isles and there are no disturbances in sight.

The 1015 isobar is well to the north. Pressure is high in the Channel and over Brittany.

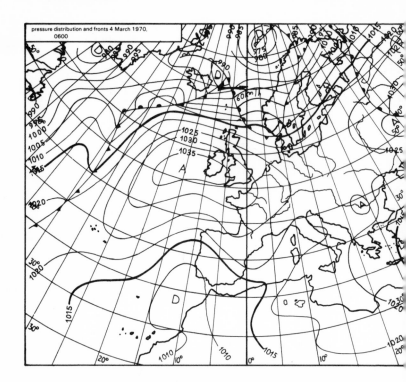

pressure distribution and fronts 4 March 1970. 0600

It is fine, slightly misty weather.

Wind mainly easterly, quite steady, from Force 2 to 3. Some coastal breezes that can produce a strong NE wind at night in Southern Brittany (Force 6 is not uncommon).

Sea flat-calm to calm.

Skies, associated with a ridge of high pressure, with altocumulus over the sea; convective clouds along the coast.

Visibility good, but slight haze on the horizon.

Outlook. This situation can develop as:

– *Unfavourable*, if the pressure gradient increases: the wind can then freshen near the coasts, in the Channel or in Ireland, and reach Force 6 during squalls; and if the anticyclone shifts east: disturbances will reappear along its

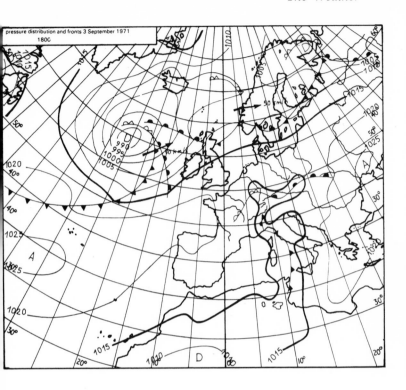

pressure distribution and fronts 3 September 1971
1800

western slope;
– *Favourable* if, quite simply, the anticyclone lasts longer than foreseen (which does happen as they only move slowly).

Ridge of high pressure lying in an east–west direction
A characteristic situation at the end of summer (September).

An anticyclonic ridge becomes established up Channel. There are no organised disturbances.

The 1015 isobar is a very long way from the Bay of Biscay, pressure is high, and its gradient slight.

Dry, slightly misty weather over the sea, cool at night and quite warm during the day.
Wind light easterly; calm in the Channel, some solar breezes.

Sea flat-calm to calm.
Skies, associated with a ridge of high pressure.
Visibility good, but possibly some fog in the morning near coasts.
Outlook. This situation can develop as:

– *Unfavourable*, if the ridge breaks down: disturbances will then cross the British Isles from north to south, often accompanied by heavy squalls;
– *Favourable*, if the gradient increases a little, bringing a wind of Force 3 to 4, clearly more pleasant for sailing.

Ridge of high pressure lying north–south

A frequent situation from May to the end of July.

An anticyclonic ridge covers the British Isles, the north of France and Spain. The disturbances pass by out in the Atlantic, and only their very much weakened edges reach the west of France.

The 1015 isobar outlines the ridge, which is very fragile (often 1018mb). The pressure gradient is therefore very slight, or we find ourselves in an area of almost uniform pressure.

Warm dry weather, calm at sea, but stormy depressions can appear in the Bay of Biscay.
Wind calm or light, from the southern sector in Brittany. Calm in the Channel. Local breezes set in.
Sea calm; a SW swell may reach the coasts.
Skies, associated with a high-pressure ridge at sea. On land, a sky of instability, cloud with stormy development daily: 'heat storms'. Skies pre-stormy and stormy (frontal thunderstorms) when cool gusts of oceanic air pass over the very warm land.
Visibility generally good, limited during squalls.
Outlook. This situation can develop as:

– *Unfavourable*, if the ridge breaks down: disturbances once more cross the British Isles; they are generally weakened,

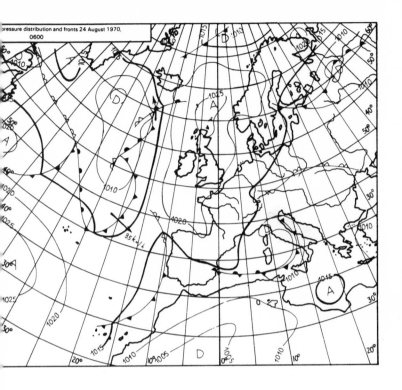

pressure distribution and fronts 24 August 1970, 0600

but their front edge is often composed of unstable warm air (cumulonimbus on the warm front);
– *Favourable*, if the ridge strengthens: the gradient increases, the wind freshens, the storm trend disappears.

Stable centres of activity, regular wind patterns, characteristic skies, well defined types of weather: it can be said that oceanic weather is above all a dependable kind of weather, without treacherous unexpected change for anyone who knows how to interpret it. Sometimes, but only rarely, it can let all hell loose, with one of those cataclysmic storms (there was a memorable one on 6 July 1969) which result from the sudden deepening of a small depression, and which play havoc locally. However, as we learn from practical forecasting, even these exceptional phenomena can be detected a few hours in advance by watching the barometer and the sky.

Generally speaking, the types of weather that appear over the Atlantic are sufficiently typical for average long-term forecasts of about a week to be valid. So it is possible to plan a cruise with some confidence. According to the position of the centres of activity, their development and the pattern and strength of the disturbances that can happen, you can work out your route. With a little flair the whole cruise can be achieved with free winds – or only going to windward in light weather. This may seem to be a timid approach but, in practice, it makes for sailing for pleasure and that is the most agreeable kind of cruise.

Weather around the British Isles and in the North Sea

The British Isles, lying on the eastern side of the Atlantic and on the western edge of the European continent, are on the receiving end of Atlantic storms. The vast majority of these storms move from south-west to north-east and, as can be seen on page 114, most of them travel over or to the north of the British Isles. It is not surprising, therefore, that the north and west experience the strongest winds. This is clearly shown in the table on pages 112–13, where Lerwick (Shetlands) and other exposed stations on the north and west coasts have the most gales. As would be expected, many more gales occur in winter than summer. However, statistics can be deceptive, and weather forecasts should be carefully scrutinised since even in the south-east and in summer, winds can reach gale force. The North Sea is sheltered to a limited extent by land on three sides but very disturbed conditions can occur as men on the oil rigs will verify.

Depressions have a tendency to be steered up the English Channel into the North Sea and also from north to south down it. The mountains of Scotland and Norway are the

Location of weather stations shown in table

Average Number of Days with Gales
(based on years 1956–1970)

TOWNS SHOWN ON MAP	JAN	FEB	MAR	APR	MAY	JUN	JLY	AUG	SEP	OCT	NOV	DEC	YEAR
Lerwick (Shetlands)	8.5	5.7	7.4	2.2	1.5	1.3	0.6	0.5	2.5	5.5	5.0	7.8	48.5
Stornoway	3.4	3.6	2.3	0.8	0.6	0.1	0.4	0.8	1.3	2.7	2.3	4.1	22.4
Wick	2.1	1.9	2.2	1.1	0.2	0.1	0.1	0.4	0.9	1.6	1.2	1.8	13.6
Kinloss	1.6	1.9	1.5	0.9	0.7	0.3	0.4	0.3	1.0	1.5	1.1	1.8	13.0
Aberdeen	1.0	0.9	1.1	0.2	0.3	0	0.1	0	0.6	0.6	0.4	0.3	5.0
Leuchars	1.5	1.5	1.7	0.5	0.6	0.4	0.1	0.3	0.7	0.9	0.9	1.5	10.6
Edinburgh	1.7	1.9	1.1	0.5	0.5	0.4	0.1	0.2	0.6	0.7	0.6	1.3	9.6
Acklington	2.3	1.9	1.5	0.5	0.3	0.3	0	0.3	0.7	0.9	1.4	1.5	11.6
Whitby	1.3	0.7	0.1	0.2	0	0.1	0	0.1	0.2	0.3	0.6	0.3	3.9
Norwich (Coltishall)	0.4	0.3	0.1	0.1	0	0	0	0	0.1	0.3	0.4	0	1.7
Ipswich (Wattisham)	0.2	0.3	0.2	0.2	0	0	0.1	0	0.1	0.1	0.3	0.5	2.0
London (Heathrow)	0.3	0.1	0.2	0	0	0	0	0.1	0.1	0.3	0.2	0.4	1.7
Dungeness	3.3	1.9	0.8	0.5	0.3	0.2	0.2	0.5	1.3	1.9	3.7	3.7	18.3
Tiree	6.4	4.3	4.0	1.3	0.7	0.4	0.3	0.9	1.8	3.4	4.5	6.0	34.0

Station													Year
Glasgow	1.0	0.6	0	0.2	0.1	0.4	0	0	0.1	0.1	0.1	1.1	3.7
Carlisle	0.6	0.2	0.3	0.2	0.1	0	0	0	0	0	0.2	0.4	2.0
Ronaldsway	4.7	4.1	2.4	1.7	0.7	0.9	0.4	0.7	1.7	3.2	3.9	5.1	29.5
Blackpool	1.5	1.0	1.2	0.5	0.6	0.1	0.6	0.6	0.9	0.8	1.3	1.2	10.3
Valley	4.4	3.3	2.1	1.3	0.8	0.6	0.2	1.1	2.2	3.6	3.9	5.1	28.6
Liverpool (Speke)	1.6	1.1	0.4	0.5	0.3	0	0.1	0.3	0.5	0.3	1.1	1.4	7.6
Aberporth	4.0	3.5	2.3	1.3	0.5	0.1	0.3	0.7	0.9	1.0	2.6	3.7	20.9
Cardiff (Rhoose)	2.1	1.1	0.1	0.7	0.7	0.3	1.6	0.6	0.7	0.6	0.6	2.6	11.7
Newquay (St Mawgan)	1.9	0.9	0.6	0.5	1.4	0.1	0.2	0.1	0.4	0.6	0.2	0.2	7.1
Exeter Airport	1.4	0.6	0.9	0.7	0.2	0.1	0.1	0.3	0	0.5	0.6	1.9	7.3
Bournemouth (Hurn)	0.3	0.2	0.3	0	0	0	0.1	0	0	0.1	0.3	0.3	1.6
Plymouth (Mt Batten)	2.5	1.8	1.2	0.5	0.5	0.7	0.1	0.3	1.0	1.4	2.6	3.1	15.7
Isles of Scilly	4.0	3.0	1.9	1.9	1.1	0.2	0.5	0.7	1.4	1.9	3.9	6.9	27.4
Aldergrove (N. Ireland)	1.5	0.5	0.2	0.2	0.1	0.2	0	0.1	0.4	0.3	0.7	1.0	5.2
Jersey (Channel Islands)	1.4	0.9	1.3	0.9	0.5	0.2	0.5	0.7	0.3	1.4	2.3	2.4	12.8

Some of the data were derived from stations near but not in the towns named

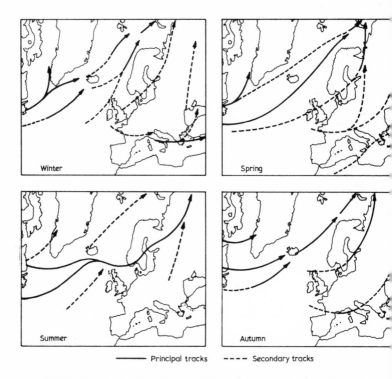

——— Principal tracks   - - - - Secondary tracks

Depression tracks (1876–1954). The winter months are December–February, spring March–May, summer June–August, autumn September–October.

The prevailing direction of movement of systems is given by arrows. Principal tracks are those most frequently followed, and secondary ones are less frequently followed and are thus less well defined. All arrowheads end on areas where depression frequency is a local maximum and here tracks may cross, branch or merge. Locally preferred regions of genesis are shown where tracks begin, whether in regions of maximum depression frequency or not. Merging indicates maximum genesis. Movement is from left to right

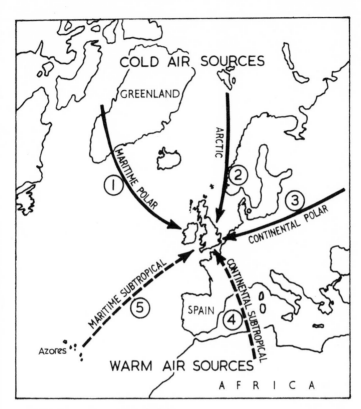

WEATHER AND AIR MASSES

Winter: 1 Showers, often squally. Rather cold. Good visibility. 2 Cold. Wintry showers, particularly near NE coasts. Mainly good visibility. 3 Very cold. Snow at times. Visibility moderate or poor. 4 Mild. Mostly dry. Moderate visibility. 5 Dull. Drizzle. Poor visibility with sea fog patches. Summer: 1 Showers, often squally. Average temperature. Good visibility. 2 Cold in north-east. Warmer in south-west. Some showers. Visibility moderate but can be poor near coasts. 3 Fine and hot. Moderate to poor visibility. 4 Warm. Sometimes thundery. Moderate visibility. 5 Dull and drizzly in south-west. Dry and warm in north-east. Moderate to poor visibility with sea fog patches in the Channel and south-west approaches

main obstacles to air movement. Winds from the north-west and south-east are funnelled by these and are particularly strong. In extreme conditions, north to north-west gales in the North Sea can lead to abnormally high tides around the coasts of eastern England and the neighbouring continent.

Air masses

The properties of an air mass, and hence the weather, depend on where it originated and what has influenced it on its passage. The chief influences are land, sea and mountains. Thus air masses arriving from north, west and south have travelled over the sea and are called maritime air masses, whereas those from remaining areas are known as continental air masses. Continental air masses are modified as they travel over the North Sea and English Channel. The principal air masses and their characteristics are shown on page 115.

The weather around the British Isles and in the North Sea depends on the pressure pattern predominating. Disturbed weather is usually associated with depressions or low pressure areas and settled weather with anticyclonic activity. In general, depressions are more mobile than anticyclones. Occasionally a well established anticyclone will block the eastward progress of a depression. This not only results in the unsettled weather being held up but often in a marked increase in wind in the 'battle' area between the two systems. The weather in and around the British Isles will be illustrated by a series of typical situations divided into disturbed patterns, settled patterns and blocking patterns.

Routine forecasts issued by meteorological offices paint a broad picture of the weather. In some areas a marked funnelling of the wind by the surrounding land occurs, and allowances should be made accordingly. Examples of this are the funnelling of air through the Straits of Dover and a marked funnelling in a north-north-westerly in the sea area between south-west Scotland and Northern Ireland, as many passengers on the Stranraer–Larne ferry will know.

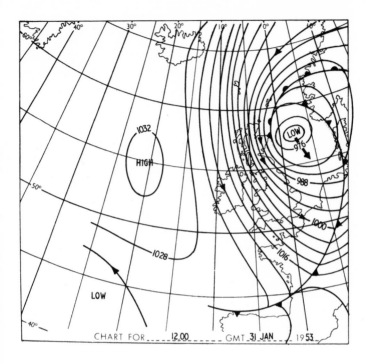

CHART FOR 12.00 GMT 31 JAN 1953

Disturbed patterns

The probable future movement of the pressure centres is indicated by a broad arrow.

Depression moving south-eastwards down the North Sea

This is an extreme case. The deep depression in the northern North Sea at 1200 GMT had moved to the German Bight by 1800 GMT and the severe gales or storm force winds spread down the western side of the North Sea. Abnormally high tides could be expected down the coasts of eastern England and adjacent continent.

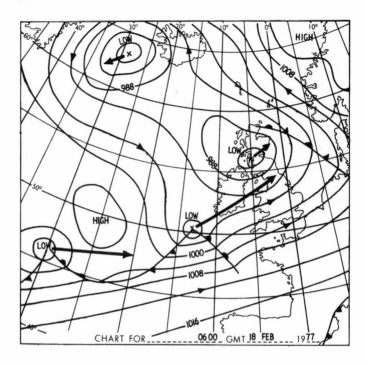

CHART FOR 06.00 GMT 18 FEB 1977

A train of depressions

At times, depressions reach the British Isles from the Atlantic at regular intervals, often 24 hours. These are known as a family or train of depressions, with each member of the family travelling on a more southerly track than its predecessor. This example shows three depressions but there are more further west.

There will be only a short period of quieter weather on the passage of the cold fronts. There is a blocking anticyclone over Scandinavia and this, together with the Norwegian mountains, is causing strong south-east winds in the northern North Sea. Sea fog is likely in the Channel and Irish Sea in the moist south-westerlies.

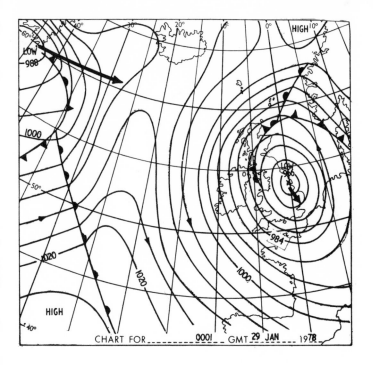

CHART FOR _ _ _ _ _ _ _ _ _ 0001 _ _ GMT 29 JAN _ _ _ 1978

Slow moving depression over eastern England with severe gales
Severe gales associated with this deep depression will be slow to moderate. They will be particularly severe in the west. The secondary depression south-east of Greenland will run south-eastwards round the main depression.

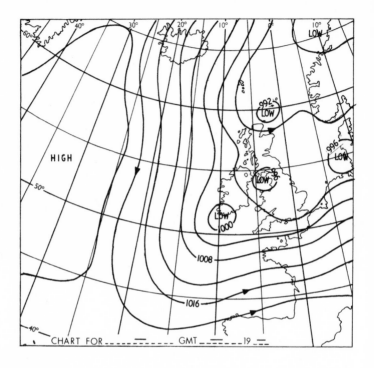

CHART FOR _____ GMT _____ 19 __

Polar depressions

In winter when a cold unstable northerly airstream affects the eastern Atlantic, shallow depressions form and move south to south-east. Winds do not usually reach gale force, though they can be strong. These depressions bring wintry weather, particularly to coastal areas.

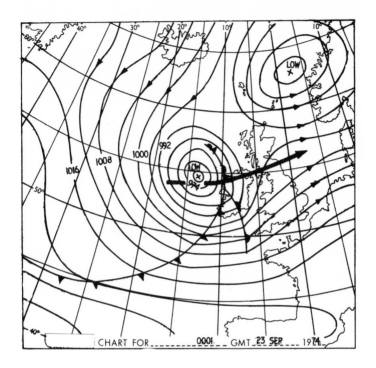

CHART FOR _ _ _ _ _ _ _ _ 0001 _ _ GMT _23 SEP_ _ _ 1974_

Secondary depression: severe funnelling in the north Irish sea behind it

The deepening secondary depression off north-west Ireland will swing round the primary off south-west Norway and move across the northern North Sea. Gales in the south will spread to many other areas and will become particularly severe behind the depression as the wind veers north-westerly. Severe funnelling will occur in the north Irish Sea. It is worth noting that gales can become severe and the winds squally in the unstable air on the backside of a depression.

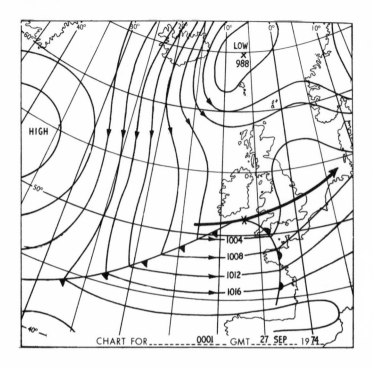

CHART FOR .... 0001 ... GMT ... 27 SEP ... 1974

Gales in Biscay and Channel spreading to southern North Sea associated with secondary depression moving across southern England

A favoured track for depressions is up the Bristol Channel. Before it turns to the left, this deepening depression will spread west-south-westerly gales up the Channel to the southern North Sea, with funnelling. Sea and swell will be high and weather in Biscay very disturbed.

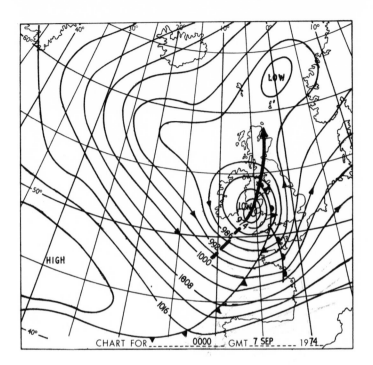

CHART FOR _____ 0000 ___ GMT 7 SEP ___ 1974

Deep depression in Irish Sea moving north-east

After the summer lull, the reappearance of disturbed weather often occurs in September – the well known autumnal gales. This is a good example. Gales, probably severe, already occurring in the south-west approaches, the Channel and Biscay will rapidly spread to the North Sea as the deepening depression moves north-east and turns to the left towards the Moray Firth. The gales will be particularly severe as the wind funnels through the Straits of Dover.

To the west of the British Isles, unstable polar air will bring squally showers to many areas with possibly more general rain as the trough of low pressure to the north-west of Ireland swings south-east behind the depression.

Settled weather patterns

Three examples of settled weather patterns are illustrated on pages 125–7. Anticyclones can be divided into two categories. Cold anticyclones form on the cold side of the polar front and, like ridges of high pressure, are usually mobile and give only a short period of settled weather. Warm anticyclones on the other hand are slow moving and more permanent. Fog can form at night overland in the light winds associated with anticyclones and may drift out to sea. It usually soon disperses. The four maps below give the main anticyclonic tracks.

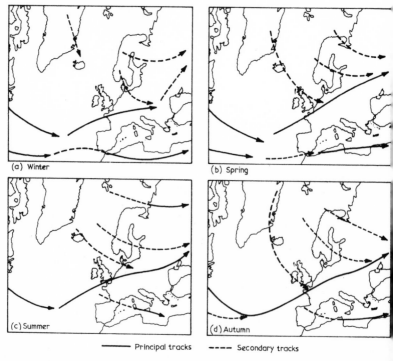

(a) Winter

(b) Spring

(c) Summer

(d) Autumn

——— Principal tracks   - - - - Secondary tracks

Anticyclone tracks, 1876–1954

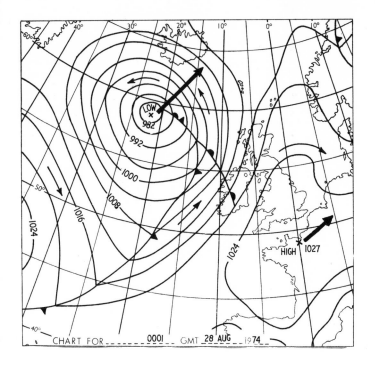

CHART FOR _ _ _ _ _ _ _ 0001 _ _ GMT _28 AUG_ _1974_ _

Warm anticyclone with blocking

The anticyclone over France is a warm one and hence will be slow moving. It is likely to prevent the rain associated with the cold front penetrating further than the Irish Sea. It can be confidently forecast that the fine quiet conditions will continue over England except the extreme north-west. Fog may form overland at night and drift over the sea, but will soon disperse.

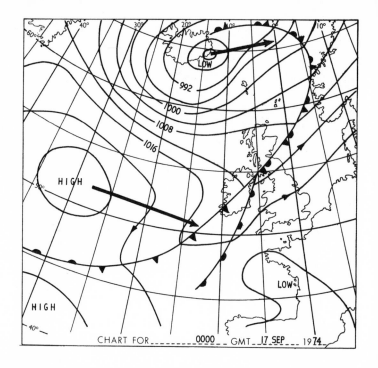

CHART FOR _____ 0000 __ GMT _ 17 SEP ___ 1974

Cold anticyclone

The anticyclone in the central Atlantic will move steadily eastwards and bring fine weather to most areas except the extreme north. Note that this is a cold anticyclone and therefore the fine quiet weather will be short lived. Look out for the next Atlantic disturbance.

The depression south-east of Iceland is interesting. The strongest winds are on its south side and these will tend to steer it eastwards.

Over Biscay there is a trough of low pressure and, although little wind, thunder storms are likely to break out and whip up the wind and sea.

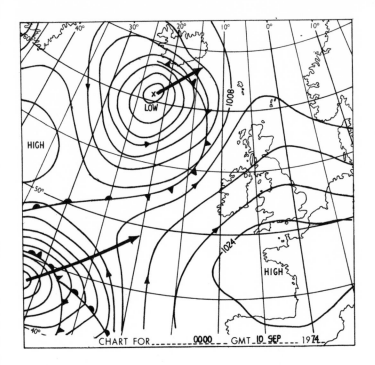

CHART FOR .... 0000 ___ GMT 10 SEP ___ 1974

Ridge of high pressure

The ridge of high pressure over the United Kingdom will move east and the fine relatively quiet weather will spread across the North Sea. The calm will be short lived as the secondary depression north-west of the Azores will bring backing and freshening winds to the south-west approaches as it swings north-east round the primary depression.

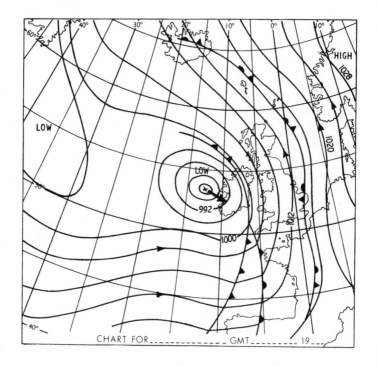

CHART FOR _____ GMT _____ 19 ___

Blocking weather patterns

In the example given, the blocking lies to the east of the British Isles but anticyclones can remain stationary in any longitude. The blocking is more likely overland in winter than in summer.

Blocking anticyclone

In winter, pressure usually builds up over Siberia and an intense anticyclone develops blocking the eastward movement of Atlantic depressions. Winds increase in the area where the depression battles to move east and in winter rain from the Atlantic turns to snow as it encounters the cold continental air flowing round the anticyclone. The example is based on weather maps for the 1978/79 winter.

Mediterranean weather

The Mediterranean has a reputation of being an area apart, where the weather does not stick to the rules. The yachtsman familiar with the Atlantic coasts, expert in observing the indications there that usually precede changes, can feel let down by the sky. In the Gulf of Lions on the French south coast, for instance, he meets gales that no cloud has foreshadowed, or when a front of good-natured appearance, stationary for days, suddenly wakes up and becomes very active.

He would be wrong however to deduce from this that he ought to forget all his previous knowledge and revise all his theories. In fact, the meteorology of the Mediterranean is not all that different and all the fundamental laws given in the preceding chapter remain valid there and in all parts of the world. The phenomena that occur are not peculiar. If they sometimes take a rather surprising turn it is entirely due to the following natural causes:

– The Mediterranean is an enclosed area with its own waters and its own sky – a character that outside influences never succeed in eliminating completely;
– All round this sea, the contrasts in temperature are considerable and they make the circulating air masses very changeable;
– Last and not least, along the coasts the land height is very varied. This causes the very special local phenomena that mask the overall situation.

To understand Mediterranean weather, particular attention must be given to its peculiarities and it is important first of all to see them in their context. We will first make a quick survey of the overall conditions: the air masses and the centres of activity controlling them, and the general patterns that emerge at different seasons. Then we will go into the detail of the western end which is of immediate interest to most yachtsmen in these waters.

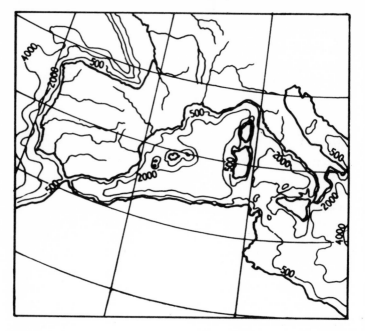

The Mediterranean is a real reservoir of heat for two reasons: the height of the surrounding mountains and the shallowness of the Straits of Gibraltar (450m)

Limits of the Mediterranean climate

The general picture

First, one basic fact: the waters of the Mediterranean and the Atlantic are very different, particularly from the thermal point of view. The water temperature of the vast Atlantic depths is in the order of 0° to 12°C, and in the Mediterranean between 10° and 13°C. This accounts, to a great extent, for the way in which the air masses, which arrive over the Mediterranean, develop.

Air masses

These air masses originate in widely different areas and are influenced by the conditions they have passed through: masses of cold air coming down from the Poles and of warm air coming up from the Tropics have different characteristics according to whether they have been over oceans or continents. When they pause over the Mediterranean, they are modified still more as a result of local conditions, and so much so that we must add a new type to our list: the Mediterranean air masses.

The occurrence and behaviour of all of them vary from one season to the next.

In winter. Some of the *maritime polar air masses* that reach the Mediterranean have first come down from Greenland to the Azores, and in the course of the journey have been well heated and loaded with humidity; others, also originating in the neighbourhood of Greenland, have taken a short cut across France and are, therefore, less warm and moist. Some, less commonly, come directly from the Arctic. They have all come very quickly and are still very cold when they arrive. In all cases, these air masses, warmed from below by the ocean, are already unstable and become more so, in varying degrees, when they approach the warmer Mediterranean. Their arrival is often announced by the cumuliform clouds forming over the coast line.

The *continental polar air masses*, which cover vast stretches of land in winter (from Scandinavia to the Balkans and the plateaux of Asia Minor), are originally stable but they also become unstable when they enter the Mediterranean area; nevertheless they are not very humid and do not generally create large cloud formations.

The characteristics of *Mediterranean air masses* depend on the temperature of the surface waters; this is in the order of 13°C to 16°C, from November to March. The sea, being warmer than the lower layers of the atmosphere, the latter are warmed and become heavy with humidity. It follows that air masses over the Mediterranean are unstable, and favourable to the development of cumuliform clouds. They are very much like the air masses of the tropical regions of the Atlantic.

In summer. *Maritime polar air masses* reach the Mediterranean less frequently. When they do arrive, having been well warmed on their journey, they have a noticeably unstable character which systematically triggers off stormy conditions.

The *continental polar air masses* remain stationary over the extreme north of Eurasia. Nevertheless, the pressure distribution is such that a regular airstream is established from the polar regions to the central and eastern Mediterranean: these are the *Etesian winds*. The cold air, passing over the extremely hot plains of Eurasia, becomes very hot and dry. Reaching the much cooler surface of the sea, an inversion of temperature occurs and produces great stability to the lower layers. There is fine, stable weather.

The *maritime tropical air masses* reach the Mediterranean in a highly developed state. They occur only at the western end and can be compared with warm maritime polar air. They are unstable.

All these types of air masses are now familiar to us, but we shall describe in a little more detail the *continental tropical air masses* (Saharan air). They do not occur in winter but they appear over the sea specially in spring. This is very hot, very dry air, loaded with dust; as a result of cooling from below there is an inversion of temperature and therefore great stability in the lower layers.

It is hot Saharan air that produces the steadiest and long-lasting winds, good for sailing, but accompanied by rather disagreeable cloudy conditions if the influx of hot air is great.

The clouds characteristic of this hot air are:

– altocumulus floccus and castellanus, at the beginning;
– stormy altocumulus at several levels follow;
– sometimes high cumulonimbus;
– stratus and fog at night and in the morning.

In summer, this Saharan type of air (which also originates in Asia Minor, the Balkans and even Spain) is present over almost all areas bordering the Mediterranean, but extends only a little out to sea for several reasons:

– A strong monsoon airstream is established towards the centre of Africa and then air flows from the Mediterranean Sahara-wards.
– The same phenomenon occurs, but on a larger scale, with the Asian zone. The winds flowing from the sea towards the deserts being the selfsame Etesian winds already mentioned.
– The 'Saharan' air originating in the Balkans or Turkey is caught up in the Etesian airflow and mixed with air, a little less warm, of continental polar origin.
– The 'Saharan' air which forms over the Iberian peninsula is an isolated nucleus which only persists if there is a general flow from the south, and it then tends to spread over western Europe rather than the Mediterranean. If the general flow is NW, the warm continental Iberian air is pushed rapidly upwards.

As in spring, when these very unstable air masses enter the Mediterranean (which happens most frequently at the end of summer and occur at the eastern rather than the western end) they become very stable in the lower layers. They then produce fog and stratus on the coasts of Libya and as far east as Malta. However, they pick up moisture at altitude and remain very unstable; if polar air comes in at the same time, there is a systematic series of violent storms, sometimes with very high cloud bases.

The *Mediterranean air masses* have almost the same characteristics in summer and winter: they are unstable in the lower layers. But in summer, if they have passed over the continent before stagnating over the Mediterranean, temperature inversion takes place in the lower layers (because the sea is not as warm as the land) which prevents any convection movement starting. On uneven levels of the coast, on the other hand, cumuliform formations are often more conspicuous than in winter.

Action centres

Over the Atlantic areas, the pressure field appears on the whole to be well organised. The lines of equal pressure surround, in clear patterns, the depressions and anticyclones and centres of activity which cover vast areas. In the Mediterranean, nothing is quite so clear. There is no permanent anticyclone, like the one over the Azores. The activity centres are greatly reduced and are often only transitory. The analysis of the pressure field becomes therefore

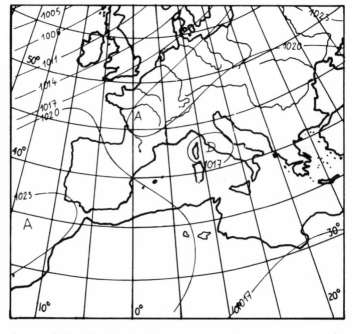

Average isobar situation in winter

generally much more complex. Nevertheless, the principal activity centres which govern the weather over the Atlantic are also playing an important part.

In winter. The Azores anticyclone does not go further north than the 40th parallel and the area of depressions off Iceland comes down to very low latitudes. The Siberian anticyclone stretches over the continent, a ridge extending it towards the west as far as the Alps. This ridge frequently disappears when the disturbances of the polar front penetrate as far as the Mediterranean.

A depression becomes established over the Tyrrhenian Sea (between Italy and Sardinia) resulting from other depressions of both local and Atlantic origin (but an anticyclone can replace them from time to time). Other small depressions occur in particular parts of the Mediterranean: the Balearic Islands, Gulf of Genoa and the Aegean.

The Siberian anticyclone is the only stable centre of activity. The other contours of the average winter isobar patterns are associated with other, very varied, conditions.

The weather is variable over the western Mediterranean basin, with dominating NW airstreams over the Gulf of Lions, westerly airstreams between Corsica and Tunisia, and southerly airstreams between the Gulf of Sidra (off Libya) and the Aegean.

Over the Adriatic there is somewhat less variable weather, owing to the predominance of a cold NE airstream.

In summer. The Azores anticyclone develops northwards. However, its eastern part collapses from time to time, letting in disturbances of Atlantic origin, which can, although weakened, reach the Mediterranean.

The result for the western Mediterranean is a variable pattern, subject to disturbances from the polar front, the dominating flow being NW and weak, which does not rule out violent tempests from all directions.

At the same time there is over eastern Europe a barometrically flat area, which is also subject to disturbances from the polar front.

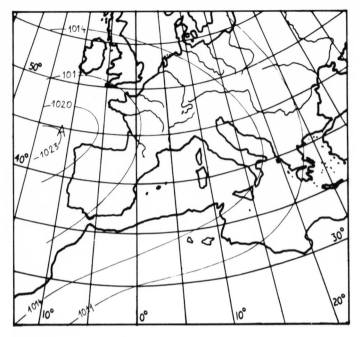

Average isobar situation in summer

A vast depression links the Asian and African sub-tropical regions. The appearance of this depression in summer is systematic and long-lasting. The lowest pressures are situated in the Persian Gulf area. The result, over the eastern end of the Mediterranean, is the very regular and permanent N and NE flow of the Etesian winds (this flow is linked with the summer monsoon of the Indian Ocean, which is itself governed by the central-Asian depression, and behaves with the same regularity). The stormy disturbances of the European barometric flat area do not overflow much into the stream of Etesian winds, where there are excellent sailing conditions. In the middle of summer, this flow can affect both the Adriatic and the Tyrrhenian Seas.

Disturbed patterns

Disturbed weather patterns generally become established in the Mediterranean in the winter months; but there are exceptions, principally in the north of the western end (the Gulf of Lions, the Ligurian Sea, the Tyrrhenian Sea).

The disturbances coming from the polar front, as has just been mentioned, reach the western end mainly in winter and spring. They are not uncommon in summer, but they are slight and it is their wake (NW squalls of wind) that is noticeable. In winter they can be very active, as the Mediterranean air masses revive the warm fronts. The disturbances can last for several days at a stretch, bringing heavy winter rains and often NW gales. The incursions of cold air that follow them

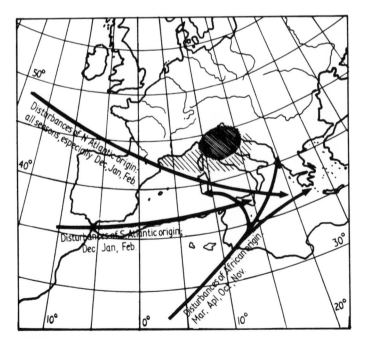

Principal tracks of disturbance and areas of cyclogenesis

give rise, at all seasons, to the Mistral and the Tramontana, famous winds of which we shall have more to say later.

Sometimes there are other disturbances that come from the Azores and the shores of Morocco. They particularly affect the African coastline, then the eastern Mediterranean. They do not lead to storms, unless they interfere with the disturbances that originate from the North Atlantic; but they almost always precipitate a lot of rain. Their normal season is December, January and February.

The disturbances of African origin are born on the edges of the Saharan area, when there is a depression over it and when there is an incursion of cold air after the passing of an Atlantic disturbance. These conditions arise in spring when the Sahara is already very hot, or in autumn when it is still very hot. These disturbances move slowly and unpredictably and their activity is moderate. They can affect any area of the Mediterranean but mainly its central and eastern regions.

Finally these 'areas of cyclogenesis' are noted at all times of the year for the small depressions they tend to form and which invite disturbances from elsewhere, the most common being the area that extends from the Gulf of Genoa to the Tyrrhenian Sea and to the north of the Adriatic. In these areas the pressure gradient is usually steeper, and consequently the winds are more violent, than elsewhere.

Anticyclonic patterns
Anticyclonic patterns become established:

- In summer, when the Azores anticyclone spills over into Europe and the western Mediterranean.
- In winter, when a continuous band of high pressure extends from the Azores to the Sahara and Eurasian anticyclone areas. The situation is then stable and lasts for several days.
- In any season (and frequently in summer at the western end) when moving ridges cross the Mediterranean region.

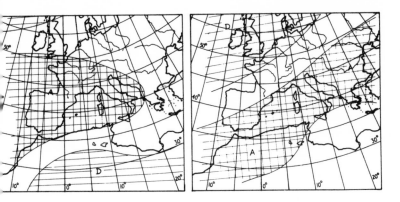

(*left*) Stable anticyclone situation in summer; (*right*) stable atmospheric situation in winter

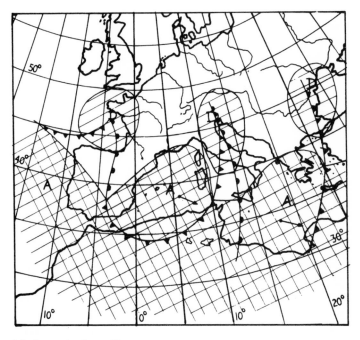

Moving anticyclone ridge

The weather throughout the year according to popular tradition
For lack of statistics linking the weather patterns to the different times of year, we are going to trust to the traditional indications, which form a fair guide. It must be used with caution, popular belief being probably ready to accept heavenly phenomena but not meticulous enough about dates. To use the main features of this guide discrepancies of up to three weeks must be allowed for and heavy weather may only amount to a local storm. But with all its deficiencies it gives useful indications. It covers only the western Mediterranean.

Early summer. The summer gradually sets in from May on. The NW storms become less and less frequent and do not last, but they remain frequent until mid-June.

High summer: mid-June to mid-August. The weather is fine, the storms are anomalies which make people comment: 'It's a wretched summer.' The Mistral occurs infrequently and does not last long but can still be very strong.

The end of summer. It begins with the 'mid-August' storm, which has the reputation of being violent. A disturbed period follows, almost cold, lasting for a week to a fortnight. It rains, the wind is variable. Then 'summer returns'. It is not so hot as in July, but the weather is reputed to be more stable. The winds at sea are slight, the coastal breezes consistent.

The autumn storm. It is reputed to take place at the end of September or the beginning of October and it is said to begin with a violent SW blow: 'the weather goes haywire' for several weeks.

Winter bad weather. It occurs between mid-November and mid-January. A succession of classic storms, often violent.

Fine winter weather. There is always a reputed stable period, of a fortnight to a month, between mid-January and mid-March; but February is said to have at least one bad ten-day patch, which sometimes spills over into March. Here we are concerned with the lively days that February has lent to March.

Spring. In April and the beginning of May, the weather becomes mild again, but it often rains.

These ridges settle behind incursions of cold air, in between disturbances.

All these situations, as in the Atlantic, are characterised by fine weather, with little or no wind. But in contrast to what happens in the Atlantic, fogs and low cloud are infrequent, except along the African coastline and in the northern Adriatic.

Conditions vary within the various parts of the anticyclone:

– In its eastern part, the winds are slight and in the NW sector, on the open sea, not very good for sailing. In contrast, the coastal breezes are quite strong and have their own characteristics which we shall discuss later on.
– In its central part the weather is less agreeable. The sun is often hidden by nearly continuous layers of stable clouds (suspended stratocumulus), especially at sea. There is virtually no wind, but near the coasts the breezes, although faint, are regular.

The western end is the region of the SE, South and SW winds at sea. On the coasts, the breezes are light or nonexistent. The weather is warm and sunny. At sea, the wind is light or moderate but, the sea not being disturbed, you have easy conditions for sailing and you can make good progress.

When the anticyclonic situation is the result of a moving ridge, one must never forget that bad weather is never very far away. Besides, it is often heralded by its 'ambassador', cirrus, that we have already seen in other skies.

Regional winds

In the course of this general analysis, some of the peculiarities of Mediterranean weather have cropped up: rapid change due to the presence of very diverse air masses, great variety of pressure, unpredictable centres of activity and complicated wind patterns. The essential feature, however, remains to be described – the winds that appear not so much complex as plain anarchical to yachtsmen accustomed to regular Atlantic patterns.

In fact, the different airstreams which approach the Mediterranean are not unusual in themselves; if they become so it is because of the very patchy and steep coastline which borders the greater part of it. Forced to rise above the mountain masses or to whistle down the valleys, the winds take on quite different characteristics from one place to the next. In the Mediterranean, to speak of a NW or SW wind means nothing: each wind has its own name, defining its direction and its character. There are several dozen of them.

There are too many to discuss even if we knew them all. After a few facts concerning the topography and its overall influence, we shall just examine the main regional winds and patterns of coastal breezes in the western Mediterranean.

Influence of topography. The Mediterranean is isolated from the surrounding areas by important mountain masses: in the west the various Spanish ranges and the Pyrenees; in the north the Massif Central, the Alps and the Balkans; in the east, the plateau of Asia Minor and the Lebanon; in the south, the chains of the Atlas and the Saharan plateau.

There are four narrow entrances through these mountains: the Straits of Gibraltar to the Atlantic, the Lauragais shelf towards the Bay of Biscay, the Rhône–Saône corridor towards Europe, and the Dardanelles–Bosphorus corridor towards the Black Sea. Elsewhere, from Tunis to Alexandria, the flat coast opens directly on to the African deserts.

In the middle of this region we find still more mountains, the Apennines, which stretch along the whole length of Italy and mark the limits of the western and the eastern Mediterranean.

Behaviour of cold air. All these mountains' masses, even the lowest, form important barriers to the movement of the lower layers of the atmosphere. They do not interfere very much with the warm air masses, which usually circulate high up, but they stop or impede the cold air masses, especially (and this frequently happens) when the latter are not very

Typical Föhn wind effect

thick. The following reaction then occurs: the cold air, forced to rise up the slopes, cools by expansion. If it is moist, it causes heavy precipitation on the windward slopes; then, having lost some of its humidity, it warms rapidly while it descends the leeward slope, and arrives at the foot of the mountain considerably warmer. This is the classic Föhn effect, which we analysed in detail on pages 18–24 to illustrate the different states of the air.

This Föhn effect occurs over the western end of the Mediterranean on each incursion of maritime polar air. The cold air does not necessarily become very warm, nor is the sky necessarily clear, but nevertheless the reputation of the Côte d'Azur for its blue sky and mildness is largely due to this occurrence. In short, the nature of the land which allows the warm air masses to penetrate and limits the effects of the cold air masses, is the physical background of the privileged climate the region enjoys.

But it is a privileged climate only to a certain extent, for the four entrances we have mentioned above must be taken into account. Far from being obstacles to the cold air, it pours through them, and its action is increased by a 'corridor effect' between the mountains. This is why Gibraltar, the Dardenelles and especially the Gulf of Lions are areas of violent winds and frequent storms.

All these influences are found again on a local scale. In detail, the terrain that borders the coast is broken up by valleys alternating with mountains. The cold air finds an outlet in each one of these valleys. Thus all along the coast there are very special winds which have only remote connections with the synoptic wind. Their general flow is very turbulent and they blow irregularly in squalls, sometimes with up and down currents.

The ground surface does not need to be very high for these aberrant winds to rise, nor for the corridors to be very distinct for them to become violent. They can happen along the north coasts of Corsica or any small, mountainous island.

Between each small valley is a col down which the wind rushes furiously (there is even a considerable difference in pressure between its two slopes). If the air is sufficiently unstable, whirlwinds can even set off spectacular waterspouts, interesting enough to watch if you are not too near. Off the coast between the corridors that the wind blows down, the air is practically still. It goes without saying that one can hardly imagine worse sailing conditions.

Finally, these winds seem to be all the more sudden and violent the more local they are: the big Mistral, coming out of the Rhône–Saône corridor, is certainly easier to cope with than the 'raggiaturi' of Cape Corsica. In the same way, an influx of cold air that is limited to the very lowest layers is more dangerous than a vast movement, whose air flow is large enough to become regular in spite of the lie of the land.

Indications of cold air. In summer, as incursions of cold air are always linked to overall movements, they are predictable and are effectively foreseen by the meteorological services. But in winter they can occur very suddenly, even in very fine weather, and prediction is almost impossible. The cumulus, the cold air type of cloud, do not act as a warning system because, when they appear, the cold air influx has already begun. There can be invasions of cold air without any cloud, when it is dry.

It can be said, however, that the appearance along crests

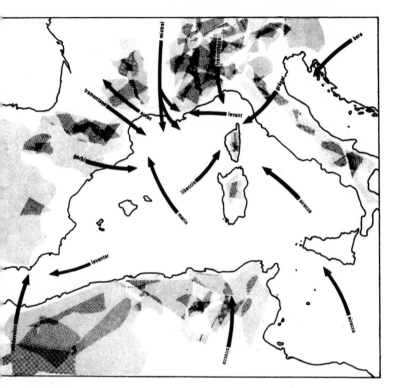

Principal local winds

or ridges and, to lee of them, of jagged cumulus, lying in long roller formations, is a sure sign of a cold, fluky and dangerous airstream: it is safer then not to go too near the coast.

The appearance of altocumulus *lenticularis* can also be regarded as indicating the arrival of cold air; but it is very rare that such an incursion occurs when middle layer clouds other than these altocumulus are in the sky.

To conclude this analysis of the relationship between the cold air and the nature of the Mediterranean land surface, it is as well to call attention to yet another phenomenon that

145

occurs on coasts exposed to influxes of warm air, in winter, when there is snow on the mountains. A cap of cold, stable air forms over the snowy surfaces and establishes a regular airstream in its lower layers towards the sea. As the cold air is very dense in comparison with the warm air, the latter cannot reach the coasts near these snow surfaces. The warm SW to SE winds are then stopped two or three miles from the coasts and a light wind blows from the land in their place. This is an important phenomenon in the interplay of coastal breezes.

After this analysis, it is pretty clear that there is a great variety of winds in the Mediterranean, and that each wind has its own characteristics. It follows that at least the more important ones must be studied individually.

Mediterranean folklore provides a unique collection of names for them. Each is quite precise, taking into account not only the area where the wind occurs, but also its direction, speed, sometimes even the characteristics of its turbulence and the effects it produces. The terminology has been largely adopted by the meteorological services and it is used in their forecasts.

The Mistral and the Tramontana

These names, from the folklore of Provence and Languedoc – Mistral and Tramontana – crop up in the forecasts for the Gulf of Lions, the Gulf of Genoa and the Ligurian Sea, all areas where these two winds often blow. They are undoubtedly the most typical of winds and, as the yachtsman has every chance of encountering them, we shall deal with them at greater length than the others.

Characteristics. The coming of the Mistral and the Tramontana is linked with the arrival of a cool maritime airstream from the Atlantic, more rarely with cold continental air coming into the Mediterranean over the Laurageais shelf and down the Rhône–Saône corridor.

In short, we have a stream of cold air strengthened at these entrances: the analysis above is also applicable here.

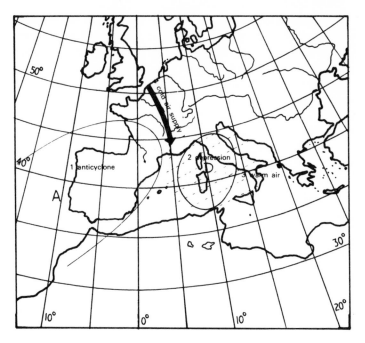

The four conditions for the appearance of the Mistral

This wind is called the Tramontana in Languedoc, Mistral in Provence and the Côte d'Azur, but it is the same wind, sometimes under other names, that occurs in the whole of the Gulf of Lions as far as the Balearics, in the Ligurian Sea, in Corsica and to the north of Sardinia. It reaches its maximum strength as it comes out of the Rhône–Saône corridor. But it can be particularly violent locally at Cape Corsica or in the Strait of Bonifaccio, for instance; and the sea is liable to be rougher off the Roussillon coast (near the Spanish frontier) than off the Camargue, further north.

The Mistral (as we shall call it from now on) blows from the north or NW on the Côte d'Azur, Provence and Langue-doc. In Corsica, it blows more from the west and only its cold-wind characteristics allow it to be differentiated from the Libeccio, a hot violent wind that also blows from the west. There are also many confused areas: in Bastia, for instance, where a marked Föhn effect takes place on the heights of the Balagne and Cape Corsica, the Libeccio is blamed for storm conditions when the Mistral is really responsible.

The Mistral is often more violent than the synoptic wind. A strength reaching 40 knots, with squalls of 60 knots, are not uncommon. It usually lasts from three to six consecutive days. But it can blow for only a few hours or, on the other hand, for 15 days on end. This last duration usually occurs during the cold season and it coincides with a disturbed NW pattern extending over the whole of western Europe. The

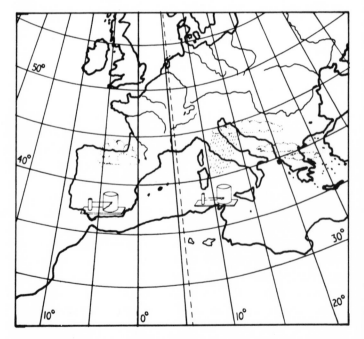

The Mistral gives a quite different warning of its approach east and west of the 6°E meridian

temporary calm periods, which are sometimes associated with the areas under the influence of these conditions, do not, however, affect the Mediterranean: the Mistral continues to blow unceasingly.

The Mistral is normally stronger by day than at night (the maximum day strength is double the minimum night strength). These variations are more evident on the coast than out at sea; they are even more evident if the sky is clear, and if the Mistral coincides with an incursion of air colder than the air that preceded it. They are in fact recognised more by their variations in turbulence than by their force.

It is as well to know that the improvement at night is only a remission, and that if you find it along the coast, you may well lose it if you take to the open sea.

The Mistral arises under these four conditions:

- The establishment of an anticyclonic ridge over SW France.
- A depression over the western Mediterranean. As the Mistral blows in the western part of this depression, it is therefore the latter's position that determines its scope.
- The presence of hot air stagnating in the zone of depression (Mediterranean air). If hot air from Africa moves into the eastern part of this depression, the weather is shocking but the Mistral is limited.
- An influx of cold air.

It is not absolutely necessary for these four conditions to be fulfilled. The third in particular is 'optional'.

The arrival of the Mistral is heralded in different ways according to location:

- To the west of the meridian 6° East: the barometer rises, rain stops, cloud diminishes and the temperature drops.
- To the east of the same meridian: the barometer drops, it rains or it has rained, the wind is moderate or light but there is a big swell.

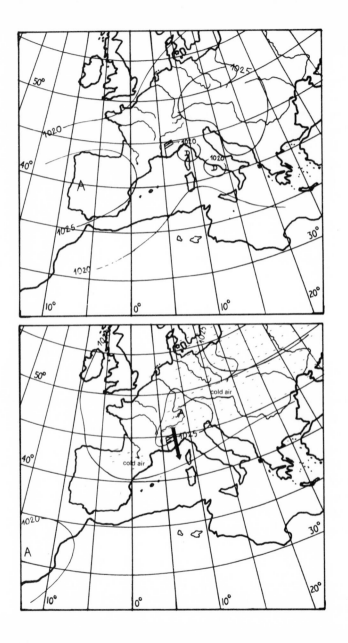

The characteristics of the Mistral vary according to how the fundamental conditions are fulfilled; there are all kinds of variations and the opinions of long-shoremen must be distrusted: in Nice for instance every cold wind is called the Mistral, even if it comes from the SW. We shall consider here four of the main types of Mistral.

The 'local' Mistral. It is limited to the Rhône Valley, the Camargue and to the north of the Gulf of Lions. Very frequent and moderate.

It is enough for only one of the fundamental conditions to exist for it to rise:

– An increase of pressure, even if not very great, from Gascony to central France;
– Or again a thermal depression in the Mediterranean, a frequent occurrence with an undisturbed pattern: a vast anticyclone covering western Europe, with only slight lowering of pressure over the Gulf of Genoa and the Tyrrhenian Sea. The Mistral then blows in the afternoon;
– In winter, in cold anticyclonic conditions over Europe, the air cooled locally by radiation is sufficient to trigger off a local Mistral, characterised by hardish squalls.

The 'white' Mistral. The Mistral is 'white' when it isn't accompanied by cloud and precipitation. This happens when the cold air is dry and stable – of continental origin. It also occurs when the Mistral arises behind a typical disturbance. The required conditions are all fulfilled, the considerable increase in pressure following the cold front gives a violent Mistral and a clear sky. This is the origin of the reputation the Mistral has of clearing the sky. This is a frequent and spectacular occurrence but it is not systematic.

(*opposite*) Two isobar situations conducive to the local Mistral. Above: increase of pressure over SW France; Below: anticyclone and cold air over Central Europe

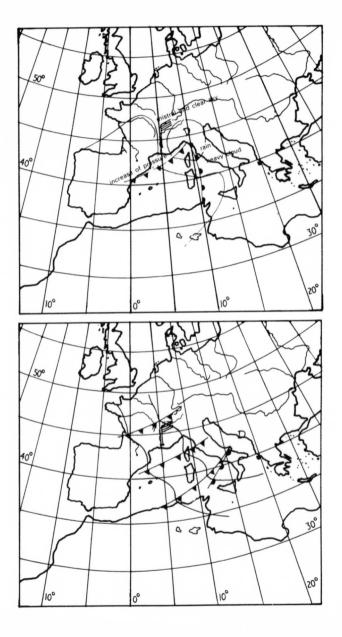

The 'black' Mistral. When cold air of maritime polar origin is moist and unstable the Mistral is 'black', as it is accompanied by a sky covered with low clouds, often backed with cumulonimbus bringing squalls. In winter it can snow.

The black Mistral occurs whenever there is no very great increase in pressure; many cold secondary fronts are passing through. Between each front, there is a brief improvement in the weather, but the wind does not abate.

It must be noted that very often the Mistral is white over Provence and the sea, while it is black over Corsica. This peculiarity is due to the Föhn effect and it can persist for several days. Seen from the coasts of Corsica, the sea is then very luminous, in strong contrast to the sky.

The ordinary Mistral. The ordinary Mistral is associated with a vast NW airstream which affects all western Europe. It occurs at all times of the year but most frequently in midwinter, and there is then a black Mistral, until the depression controlling the NW airstream has moved far enough east. The Mistral becomes white as pressure increases. The NW airstream can extend to the coast of Tunisia. The wind is strong everywhere, but more particularly in the recognised 'Mistral areas'.

The end of the Mistral. The Mistral dies down or stops altogether when the four fundamental conditions are waning. This can happen in different ways; we shall mention the two classic cases.

The Gascony anticyclonic ridge collapses and a group of disturbances of Atlantic origin moves down towards the Mediterranean. After the passage of the first disturbance, the anticyclonic ridge appears and the Mistral blows. The arrival of the second disturbance interrupts the influx of cold air. Pressure falls and the temperature becomes milder;

(*opposite*) Above: *White* Mistral; Below: *Black* Mistral

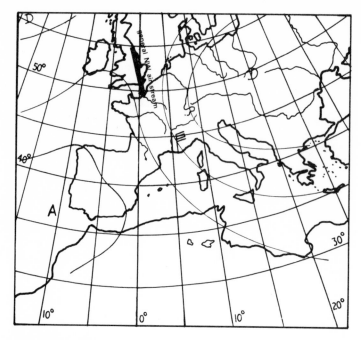

The *ordinary* Mistral

cirrus spreads over the sky, followed by middle layer clouds; the wind abates and tends to blow in a westerly or SW direction.

The end of the Mistral is accompanied by a rapid and clear improvement in the weather, but it does not last long. A new disturbance follows: first rain and SW winds, then the Mistral returns after the second cold front has passed through.

(*opposite*) Above: An *anticyclone ridge* forms behind a disturbance; the Mistral blows; Below: a second disturbance arrives: the Mistral stops but there is only a brief respite

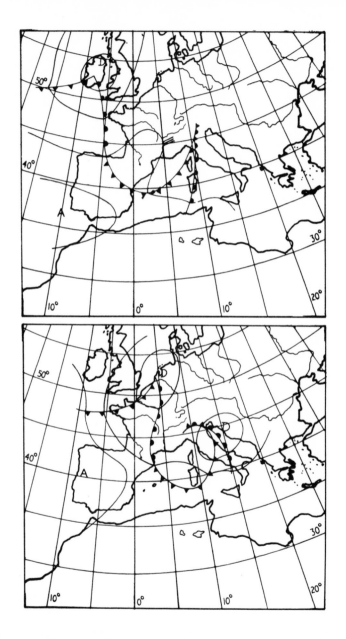

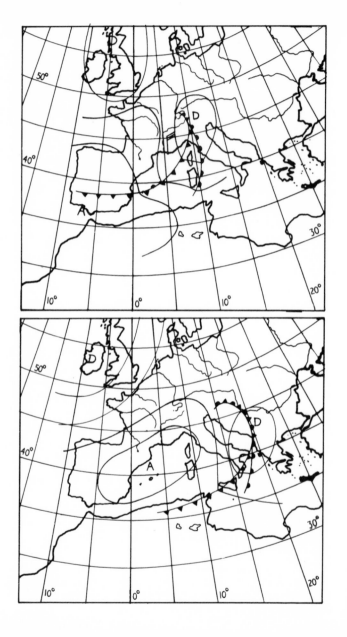

It is in these conditions that the local saying holds good: 'A short Mistral does not bring back fine weather.'

The extension of the anticyclone towards the Mediterranean. The high pressures of western Europe extend towards the south. The depression of the Gulf of Genoa and the Tyrrhenian Sea fills up or moves east. There are the beginnings of an anticyclonic pattern, and the Mistral weakens.

Note that such a situation is favourable for making a passage from Marseilles to Corsica or Sardinia: a good north wind to start with, turning to NW then west, and weakening throughout the passage. And fine weather to follow. A Mistral which persists and only abates slowly brings back fine weather.

Out of a hundred cases of the Mistral blowing at over 25 knots at sea, thirty-eight developments of the first type have been noted and sixty-two of the second type. A yachtsman cooped up in harbour by bad weather can look on the arrival of the Mistral as a happy event: he will not be frustrated much longer.

The Tramontana. It arises in the Gulf of Genoa–Tyrrhenian Sea area. The Tramontana is a north to NE wind affecting the west coast of Italy and the Tuscan archipelago, but it can also reach and even go further than Corsica.

It often follows a Mistral. After the influx of cold air over the west Mediterranean, an anticyclonic pattern sets in with the formation of a ridge of high pressure as far as the plain of the Po, while low pressures have become established and persist over southern Italy.

Rarely very violent, the Tramontana is however quite strong off Cape Corsica, when it follows hard on the Mistral. It usually affords pleasant sailing in a good breeze.

(*opposite*) Above: The last disturbance of a family has passed: the Mistral blows; Below: the anticyclone develops: the Mistral gradually dies down, for good this time

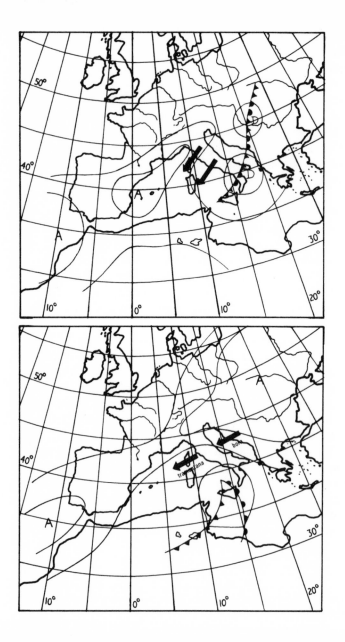

In winter, the Tramontana is often a prolongation of the *Bora*, a seasonal wind blowing over the Adriatic. It is then extremely turbulent. The pressure gradient in the lower layers is steep, an anticyclone being well established over central Europe with extension over the Alps. The cold air of Balkan origin is very dry and arrives in the Mediterranean after crossing the Apennines, without there being any Föhn effect (dry air, no precipitation). If the airstream is strong enough, it reaches and crosses the Corsican mountains. This orographic rising disorganises the stream more than it checks it, and the cold air arrives in short, violent squalls, interrupted by periods of calm. These gusts are often very localised and can be overlooked by the meteorological forecasts.

The Marin

The Marin is a mild or warm, damp wind, accompanied by rain which blows from the SE, South or SW over the Gulf of Lions and the neighbouring coasts.

It has no particular meteorological characteristics, as it corresponds to the very classic case of the rainy wind that generally occurs in advance of a warm front. It merits a special mention however since it is the opposite and almost hostile to the Mistral. Although not so strong as the latter, it raises quite a sea along the coasts of Provence, as its fetch is so long. On the coasts of Languedoc, it is allied to the *Autan*, a warm local wind.

We can recall and clarify here a remark we have already made. In winter, when conditions favour a local Mistral (cold air on land, the mountains of the Cevennes and of Provence being snow-covered), the Marin cannot reach the coast. A curious spectacle then takes place: the sky is covered with the typical clouds of a warm front, it rains, and

(*opposite*) Above: The Tramontana blows up after the Mistral; Below: The Tramontana in winter

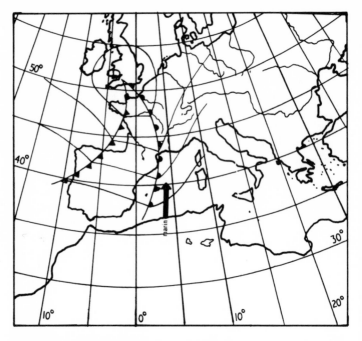

The mild and damp Marin wind is to the Mediterranean what the south-westerly is to the Atlantic

yet the Mistral, although quite weak, blows several miles out from the coasts. Go a little further out and everything changes: the wind is southerly and clearly much warmer. This is the 'lost' Marin.

The Sirocco
The Sirocco, and the other hot winds of the same family (*leveche, chili, ghibli, khamsin*) come from Africa or Asia and spread over the Mediterranean when a strong south–north airstream is established between a depression centred on the Mediterranean and a ridge of high pressure situated to the east of it. Such winds only affect clearly one part of the Medi-

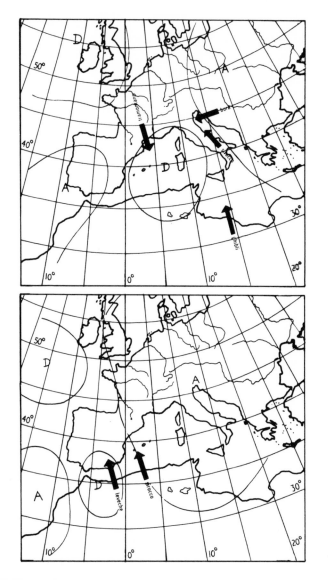

The Sirocco blows at the east or west end of the Mediterranean according to
the positions of the action centres

terranean at a time. The chosen time is spring (April or May), but they are equally common in autumn.

All these winds have the same characteristics. They are laden with dust: visibility is bad, the sky takes on a yellowish tinge, the sun is blurred. They are hot in comparison with the average temperature for the season. The air is stable in the lower layers (the sea is colder than it is), unstable at high altitude. It is dry near the coasts of Africa and becomes very moist in the lower layers as it spreads over the sea.

The result is fog and low stratus, lasting for a long time and certainly as troublesome for navigation as Channel fogs in winter.

The sky has middle layer clouds with thunderstorm characteristics, or even cumulonimbus with a very high base. Electrical charges are intense but not very dangerous at ground level. Short showers of warm muddy rain may occur, more commonly in the north of the Mediterranean than in the south, but never lasting for long and never very heavy. The wind is strong but seldom very strong. The swell is very big (for the Mediterranean) as the fetch is long and winds like this can last for several days.

In short, apart from the fog (which doesn't occur everywhere) and the swell (which has the advantage of being short, as it usually is in the Mediterranean), the conditions are quite good for sailing. The drawback is one does not benefit from the Mediterranean sun (and this is not the only occasion). If you go off eastwards, the weather improves, but you lose the wind. If you go off westwards (or the activity centres move eastwards), you get very bad weather in the western part of the depression: rain and violent storms.

There are some other regional, or rather local, winds that do not have sufficiently generalised characteristics to be described here. We will refer to them later when we recapitulate the features of the different areas of the western Mediterranean. But we must first consider one last important phenomenon: coastal breezes.

Coastal breezes

The coastal breezes are particularly strong on the Mediterranean for two reasons:

– they are linked, as we know, to sunshine, and that is considerable;
– they are strengthened by the proximity of the mountains, where a similar pattern of breezes appears: a *valley* (*or anabatic*) breeze in the daytime, a *mountain* (*or katabatic*) breeze at night.

The two types of breezes combine.

It does not appear that the synoptic wind, when it is the same direction as the breeze, is added to it. The two phenomena seem to be quite independent: in little bays it is the synoptic wind that dominates (even if it is the less strong of the two); in large bays, it is the breeze that takes over.

The sea breeze

The mechanics are always the same. The sea breeze is all the stronger and starts all the sooner, as the air over the land is more unstable. Seen out at sea, cumulus appearing over the land mass give hopes of a favourable breeze to take you landwards, even if, for the moment, the wind is weak or contrary. But an arrival of stable air (ahead of a warm front) prevents the breeze setting in even if it is very fine. The synoptic wind itself, if it blows from the sea, can find itself blocked at the opening of a bay surrounded by high mountains. This calm near the coast in summer, when it is fine, is therefore often a sign of a change in the weather.

The sea breeze starts up two to four hours after sunrise, reaches its maximum strength a little after the passage of the sun over the meridian. In good conditions it reaches 20 knots, more often 8 to 12 knots; it dies away one or two hours before sunset.

The land breeze

The land breeze is usually not so strong as the sea breeze, but it is more regular and sustained. It is capable of driving up a fairly strong synoptic wind in opposition to itself. In winter, when there is snow on the mountains, it is particularly steady and strong.

If the air over the sea is warm and unstable enough, stratocumulus and cumulus appear near the coast when a land breeze sets in.

It occurs immediately after sunset, sometimes a little before; it reaches 6 to 8 knots, sometimes 10 knots towards the end of the night; it disappears with the dawn or a little later.

Even more than with the sea breeze, the absence of a land breeze when it is fine is a sure sign of an approaching disturbance. Its absence indicates an equalisation of temperature over land and sea.

After the passage of a warm front, when the rain stops and the sky clears, even partially, the breeze reappears. But it can die during the wake's passage when the air is equally cold over sea and land.

The extensive area of the breezes

It is customary to assume that the breezes affect only a coastal band twenty miles deep. This can indeed be taken as the extreme limit; it must be reckoned from the average shore line and not from headlands. The sea breeze does not often get that far but the land breeze usually does towards the end of the night.

Naturally the play of breezes varies greatly according to the indentations of the coastline. Each little bay, inside a much larger gulf, has its own wind pattern, at least at the time when the breezes set in. When they have gathered strength these very localised winds become part of the breeze blowing along the whole coastline. This is particularly true for the land breeze which, at the beginning of the night, takes as many directions as there are small bays and valleys, and only finds a regular pattern and strength as the night goes on.

These breezes are characteristic of fine weather, and very favourable for dinghy sailing off the coast. When cruising, you know that you can count on a land breeze to leave harbour and reach open water towards the end of the night. By the same token you can take maximum advantage of the sea breeze to make a landfall on a broad reach in the early afternoon.

West Mediterranean by areas

We shall assemble here a number of tips on the sailing conditions to be found at different points in the western Mediterranean. These are only the very classic indications that give the basic knowledge that will lead you to make your own discoveries.

Languedoc, Provence, Gulf of Lions, North Balearics
When we have said this is the zone of the Mistral, we have said all. However, a few particular points call for attention.

– The NE wind is sometimes violent (if the Tramontana); it is called the *Gregale* in Provence, the *Levanter* in Catalonia and the Balearics. It is not common.
– The summer sea breeze is steady and sustained (without exceeding Force 4); it almost always becomes the predominant wind on the shore line, even when the Mistral is blowing. The latter comes again at night, out to sea.
– The land breeze often becomes integrated with the Mistral, and together they usually prevent the sailor from reaching land.

Out of a hundred cases of wind of 30 knots or more at sea, the following distribution has been recorded: Mistral-Tramontana: 88; Marin: 3; Gregale: 9. This area is where the strongest winds in the Mediterranean are recorded. At Marseilles, on average, a hundred days' Mistral a year are recorded.

South Balearics and Alboran

An area with a very Mediterranean character on the whole. In particular, it has a regular and systematic pattern of breezes on the coasts in summer but less regular in the cold season.

In winter when there is a disturbed situation with a depression centred over Oran, the wind that blows from the east and brings rain is called the *Solano.*

The area east of Gibraltar is where the Atlantic and Mediterranean influences confront each other, and result in two winds:

- the *Levanter*, an east Mediterranean wind, mild but often irregular;
- the *Vendavales*, a SW Atlantic wind, cool damp, steady. It is often accompanied by showers.

One of the characteristics of this area is that one passes suddenly from one wind to the other.

The Ligurian Sea and around Corsica

The dominant wind is the *Libeccio*, but its name does not correspond to a wind with precise characteristics. One thing is certain: it is a west to SW wind, moderate to strong, hot or mild, never excessive. It foreshadows, or is accompanied by, bad weather.

We have seen that in Corsica the Mistral blows usually from the west (or WSW), as it reaches Corsica when the depression, which is its partial origin, has moved towards the Gulf of Genoa or the Tyrrhenian Sea. The only difference between the Mistral and the Libeccio is that the arrival of the first coincides with a lowering of the temperature and often to a clearing of the sky, while the second brings mild, rainy weather. In a Mistral, one is in polar air or cold maritime Arctic air; in the Libeccio, in warm maritime polar air or Mediterranean air.

But when the wind is from the NW and brings rain, it is

also called the Mistral (really the black Mistral).

At this stage it is worth analysing in a little more detail the winds around Corsica.

Cape Corsica and the North of the Island. West winds dominate all the year round with maximum frequency in summer. The strong winds (70 per cent are westerly), caused by the frequent cyclogenisis over the Gulf of Genoa, raise a steep sea over the coast between the Gulf of Galeria (to the south of Calvi) and the extremity of Cape Corsica. In certain cases, owing to the orographic effect of the land surface of Corsica, these dominantly west winds reach Force 7 to 9 to the north of Cape Corsica over a strip of water running in a north–south direction, some ten miles wide.

The East Coast. During west winds of Force 6 to 7, the wind is light on the east coast, but between Cape Corsica and Bastia (on the lee coast) and in valley openings, it can gain strength.

As a general rule when one is sailing near this coast, watch out for violent squalls coming off the mountains, even if the west wind is only moderate.

The strength of the Mistral and the Libeccio is much weaker to the south of Bastia, between this port and Porto-Vecchio.

In summer the sea is relatively calm. East winds are rare. But when they do blow, the swell usually precedes them by a few hours.

The South Coast, Bouches de Bonifaccio. The Bouches de Bonifaccio are remarkable. Between the high rocky shores of Corsica and Sardinia, they make a passage where the wind is almost always violent. Legend has it that the monsters, Scylla and Charybdis, haunted these waters, which will hardly surprise yachtsmen who wait in the excellent port of Bonifaccio for a calm period to get through the strait.

Without over-simplifying, it can be said that in these Bouches, the wind is either west or east, that it blows either at less than 10 knots or above 40 knots. A speed of 45 knots is quite usual, even when it is very fine elsewhere.

The West Coast. As one goes northwards up the coast, the predominant winds are roughly NW. The change is very sharp at the northern limit of the sector towards the Island of Cargalo to the north of the Gulf of Porto.

Perhaps the most important conclusion this study brings us to is this: in the western Mediterranean most winds (thanks principally to the Mistral and the Tramontana) are accompanied by clear skies. The yachtsman gets no warnings and this is all the more irksome as the wind can sometimes rise in a matter of minutes and is immediately violent. Moreover, at any moment, it can change and strengthen suddenly by more than one Force. One must always be ready to change plans and be carried away east when you intended to go west or *vice versa*. Unless there is no alternative one doesn't argue with the Mistral. It raises a horrible sea, with short very hollow waves, which cut down the speed of the boat and the morale of the crew. Do not cruise against the run of the weather.

In fact, perhaps one of the delights of sailing in this sea is following and using to the best advantage the meteorological situation without trying, at all costs, to pursue a precise plan. By not hesitating to change the itinerary and to make unforeseen stops, a cruise in these waters is almost always pleasant.

A good preparation for cruising in the Mediterranean is to read Homer. When the winds are not favourable, the best course is undoubtedly to do as Ulysses did: wait patiently. But like him, one must also know how to be wily and seize an opportunity as soon as Aeolus, who was given power over the winds by Zeus, seems to be in in good humour.

4 The Weather to Come

Yesterday's weather has been experienced and recorded, enjoyed or suffered but it is not of much use today, although it may show trends. What really matters is tomorrow's weather, a somewhat unknown quantity, but which must be foreseen if a sensible course has to be worked out – tactics if and when bad weather comes.

Knowledge of weather past is clearly very useful for the prediction of weather to come as it allows certain constants to be established which can be collated with the characteristic developments that are predicted. However, when it comes to determining the general picture of the weather for the next few days, you certainly cannot depend solely on personal observations, however experienced one is. The preceding analyses have demonstrated that the weather at any particular spot is only one aspect of an overall situation which lies far beyond the horizon of the observer; it is often the result of what was happening the day before, hundreds or thousands of miles away; its subsequent development depends therefore above all on how the general situation develops. This information can only be supplied by the meteorological services, whose observation network covers the world.

Personal observation comes next and it is a matter of comparing the local weather with the overall situation and trying to see, from the barometer, the sky and the state of the sea if the forecast matches up with local conditions or if the situation is developing faster or slower than was expected in the forecast or if one is heading towards worsening or improving weather.

Defined thus, the role of observation seems very modest. In practice, only years of experience enable you to reach conclusions of your own. That is also why not much advice can be given on forecasting the weather. It only comes, as we said at the beginning, from a good understanding of the weather forecasts and from immersing yourself in studying the subject. No other person can help you.

Weather forecasts

All the essential information that concerns yachtsmen is given in the weather forecasts broadcast on the radio and (if one wants to go in deeper) by the daily information that are published by most of the national meteorological services.

Marine almanacs give the stations and times of the regular shipping weather forecasts. Wherever they are broadcast they give, with some variation in detail, but in the same order, the following information:

– Warnings of possible storms, then the overall picture: characteristics of the pressure fields, locations of activity centres, the track of disturbances and the position and speed of movement of fronts;
– Area forecasts;
– General trends of the weather;
– Summary of observations taken at the different coastal stations.

All this information gives a good overall picture, in the area where one is sailing, of the general situation and of what is likely to happen in the short term. But it is important to realise the limitations.

First, there is an inevitable delay between the time when the observations have been made and when the forecasts are broadcast. A forecast broadcast at 0900, for instance, is drawn up as a result of observations made at 0100. Usually this delay is not serious but it can be if there are very rapid developments. It is worth remembering that the summaries

France I, one of the two frigates of the French Meteorological Services

of observations made by coastal stations given at the end of the forecast are usually more recent than the overall analysis (summaries at 0700 for the 0900 bulletin). These summaries deserve to be listened to with particular attention because they sometimes reveal anomalies not mentioned in the general situation report and give more exact information on what developments can take place.

Again (and this is the main limitation of the general forecast already mentioned) the information given covers enormous areas. It does not give exact information on the intensity which a particular phenomenon can take locally nor its exact timing. The intensification and weakening of a front, for instance, might not be indicated and, for a very localised area, this might greatly modify the forecast as far as you are concerned. Moreover, and especially in summer, these forecasts often have to give a variety of possibilities from which a choice must be made.

It is here, therefore, that personal observation comes in, and above all the use of the only meteorological instrument that is indispensable on board: the barometer.

The barometer

The sorcerer, as it was called by sailors of days gone by, sits quietly in its corner, with its highs and lows giving a faithful account of the comings and goings in the atmosphere.

The pressures it shows have however one significant limitation. One can easily believe that there is an anticyclonic situation if the needle reaches and goes higher than 1,020 mb, or that there is a rather depressionary area when it goes below 1,010mb (the figure for a very strong depression can be 960mb, in its centre). But it is also possible to experience bad weather with pressures in the region of 1,015mb. In any case it is a good thing for the barometer to be adjusted (calibrated) so that it indicates true pressures. We shall see that this is particularly important for forecasting dangerous conditions.

But what is of the utmost importance to watch are, in practice, the variations of the needle, which indicate *tendency*.

This term, tendency, is used by meteorologists to define

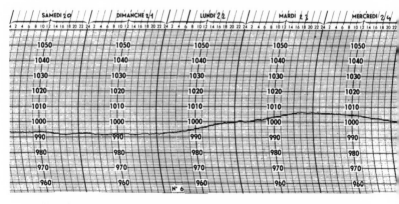

The barograph is the ideal for following changes in pressure. But it can be disconcerting

changes of pressure (higher or lower) during a period of three hours.

This is very important. Besides, in the daily weather reports (DWR) there is a map of tendencies, on which are marked lines of equal pressure change (*isallobars*). These isallobars usually take the form of ellipses merging into each other and forming centres of pressure change which generally go in couples (a centre of lowering pressure, a centre of rising pressure). Evidence of these is one of the chief concerns of weather forecasters.

For the isolated observer, this tendency is also the fundamental piece of information, for it can indicate, in the most precise fashion, a development in the weather. Generally speaking, a drop of 2 to 3mb in the space of three hours must lead one to think seriously of the possibility of worsening weather; a drop of 3 to 5mb indicates the approach of a strong disturbance; and if the drop is more than 5mb, then something quite out of the ordinary is going to happen.

But these statements need some qualifying. A tendency does not give an absolute indication; the violence of a disturbance is not exactly proportional to the negative tendency which indicates it. There can even be storms with a completely positive tendency, in a cold air stream from the NW to NE sector for instance. Most of the time, nevertheless, it is important to watch this tendency, and see if observation confirms it: a negative tendency and the appearance of a head sky usually indicate that things are going to get worse. The barometric tendency is even, sometimes, the one available fact, particularly for foreseeing dangerous conditions which slip through the meshes of the meteorological network.

Forecasting dangerous conditions

At sea, the dangerous conditions are the unexpected ones, those that surprise by their suddenness.

Among these phenomena, the one to fear most is clearly the cataclysmic freak storm, usually produced by a small

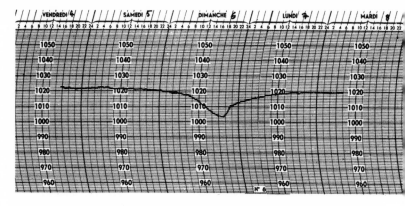

A typical drop recorded at Dinard at the time of the great storm of 6 July 1960

harmless looking depression, which suddenly deepens near the coast and does enormous damage even before the meteorological services have been able to announce the danger.

This sort of storm is fortunately rare, but not exceptional: six have been recorded in twenty years in Brittany. Two of them have taken place in summer, the one on 6 July 1969 being the deadliest of all since it caused the death of thirteen yachtsmen.

The speed with which such hurricanes develop clearly make their forecasting very difficult. They move too quickly for the swell to precede them. The state of the sky certainly makes one think that bad weather might be on the way but gives no reason to anticipate its intensity. Only the barometer can give some warning of their approach, at least a few hours in advance.

In practice, one can conclude that something serious is going to happen when one or several of the following incidents are noticed:

– The barometer falls rapidly, the tendency being more than 5mb in three hours.

– Much sooner than predicted, the pressure it indicates approaches or becomes lower than was announced by the last forecast as the centre of the depression. This means either that the depression has speeded up, or that it has deepened – or both at once.

– The pressure drops very low while the wind remains stubbornly in a SE direction, suggesting that the centre of the depression is still a long way off.

One sees here how important it is to have a calibrated barometer, because it is only by comparing the pressure given in the forecast with the one observed that it is possible to be alerted in time. It is obviously necessary to note the position of the centre of the depression, as well as its forecasted direction and speed.

It is important not to be deceived by the calm which usually settles close to the centre of a depression. During the course of the freak storm of 6 July 1969, it was observed that the wind changed a few minutes from calm to Force 12. In general we know too that the cold front of a depression is more formidable than its warm front and this was certainly the case here.

Other conditions can be dangerous in spite of being less violent. The danger with them is due not to a lack of forecasts but rather to yachtsmen not paying sufficient attention. This is especially the case for *secondary cold fronts,* against which one is not on one's guard, although they are in fact more violent than the main cold front. You must therefore be on the look out when the forecasts mention these minor fronts, and also when you notice, after a normal cold front has gone through, that the wind does not go northerly (and all the more so when it has a tendency to back slightly south, in spite of a wake sky persisting). Finally, watching the sky ought to allow one to make preparations in time, as the arrival of each one of these fronts is marked by a line of squalls consisting of cumulus congestus and cumulonimbus.

Following through the same line of thought, you must also

175

watch out for the squalls which occur in very unstable air and which sometimes bring a much stronger wind than was expected. It is not uncommon for an average wind of Force 5 to reach Force 6 or 7 in gusts.

You must be particularly on your guard in thundery conditions. Here anything can happen. For instance, the wind is weak, Force 1 to 2, heavy clouds pass over without any appreciable increase in wind and, suddenly, when you least expect it, you are in a squall of Force 6 and more . . .

As in many other fields, direct experience helps to sharpen your nose – 'once bitten, twice shy'. A good fright with a lucky outcome is worth volumes of bookish knowledge if you want to be a good weather forecaster.

Glénans, 6 July, 1969. With a fetch of some 500m, the seas rise and break in a matter of moments; the almost ubiquitous streaks of foam follow the direction of the wind. There is spray everywhere. The wind reaches Force 10

Observation

Knowing how to watch the sky and interpret it only comes after long apprenticeship. The honest observer, who is not satisfied to simulate knowledge by throwing off technical jargon, has a long haul up a steep mountain to a fount of real expertise. Only when he has drunk at it will he know how to qualify his assertions and not stand by them in the face of new developments. He will, as a matter of course:

– Take out a subscription to a meteorological journal or at least study the daily weather maps published in some newspapers.
– Listen to the weather forecasts morning and evening, look at the sky at least four times a day, and at the barometer too, then draw a forecast for the next day; and
– The next day, compare his forecast with what actually happened and analyse the discrepancies.

He will practise this exercise for several months, at different seasons.

He will then find there is really no reason to stop. If he stops, he must not in any case wait until the day before leaving on a cruise to take up his studies again. One must get back into the swing of things several days before by listening to the forecasts, consulting the maps and making contact with a coastal station to get the middle range forecasts.

Once at sea again, forecasting is based on constant observation. This is the fundamental discipline. Keep it up, day after day, and you get the habit of 'living' the weather. Unconsciously, the variations of temperature, the gradations of light and the beat of the wind are noticed and recorded. A new sixth sense is acquired which helps you on the road to reliable forecasting and you will have mastered the theory and be putting it into practice with instinctive sensitivity of the old salts.

5 Sources of Information for Practical Meteorology

In a book of permanent reference like this, only the principal sources of weather information are given for the obvious reason that publications, transmission times and so on are liable to change year by year. British nautical almanacs publish these details annually and the British and French meteorological services issue their own publications with frequencies, times, telephone numbers, etc.

In addition many British and French newspapers give daily weather bulletins and the French service (*Le Service d'Information de la Météorologie*) publishes annually in March a co-ordinated sheet with full particulars.

British reports

British yachtsmen normally receive the BBC shipping forecasts on ordinary receivers when they are in French waters and indeed these forecasts are listened to at the Glénans Sea Centres.

The BBC shipping forecasts are broadcast regularly at convenient times, the early forecast being particularly appreciated by yachtsmen because they can listen to it while they are still in their bunks; and it is a useful bulletin for this is the time for making plans. If the report is bad you are well placed to prepare for what is coming. The forecasts are given area by area, always in the same sequence. The announcer is always competent, the diction perfect and one quickly becomes familiar with the terms used. The information is given in the order below:

BBC shipping forecast

'This is the Shipping Forecast issued by the Meteorological Office at (time).'

Gale warnings

These (if any) 'are in operation for sea areas . . .' Always announced first, they give estimated times when the weather is expected to deteriorate, with wind forces for the relevant areas. Programmes are sometimes interrupted for gale warnings.

The General Synopsis

This is well worth recording for the information about depressions, anticyclones, occlusions, cold and warm fronts and so on will enable you to make better interpretations of your local weather later in the day. Air pressures are given in millibars: 'a thousand and three' or 'one, double 0 three' (1003); or 'nine, eight, five' (985). Time is given on the twenty-four clock system: 0 seven hundred = 7 am, eighteen hundred = 6 pm. (The BBC abide by British Summer Time during these months – unlike the tide tables, which are always according to Greenwich Mean Time.)

Atmospheric movements and pressures are described in the present tense: 'High 1013 is moving slowly east and weakening' for example; or 'Low 985, centred over sea area Rockall, moving eastwards at twenty-five knots and deepening, is expected 956 in sea area Forties at 0700 tomorrow'.

You will hear of 'depressions filling', 'anticyclones collapsing' and they will be doing this slowly or quickly. Other phrases you will become familiar with are 'associated fronts crossing' certain sea areas and 'high 1040 over Azores with ridge extending to the British Isles' – this last is good news for yachtsmen.

Complete beginners are reminded that, although there is a French department in Brittany of the same name, the Finisterre referred to in shipping forecasts is in Spain – corresponding with that sea area.

Beaufort scale of wind force

Beaufort Number	Description	Speed in knots*	Height of sea in feet†	Deep sea criteria
0	**Calm**	less than 1	—	Sea mirror-smooth.
1	**Light air**	1–3	$\frac{1}{2}$	Small wavelets like scales, no crests.
2	**Light breeze**	4–6	$\frac{1}{2}$	Small wavelets still short but more pronounced. Crests glassy and do not break.
3	**Gentle breeze**	7–10	2	Large wavelets. Crests begin to break. Foam is glassy.
4	**Moderate breeze**	11–16	$3\frac{1}{2}$	Small waves becoming longer; more frequent white horses.
5	**Fresh breeze**	17–21	6	Moderate waves, and longer; many white horses.
6	**Strong breeze**	22–27	$9\frac{1}{2}$	Large waves begin to form; white crests more extensive.
7	**Near gale**	28–33	$13\frac{1}{2}$	Sea heaps up; white foam blown in streaks.
8	**Gale**	34–40	18	Moderately high waves of greater length; crests begin to form spin-drift. Foam blown in well-marked streaks.
9	**Strong gale**	41–47	23	High waves; dense streaks of foam. Crests begin to roll over.
10	**Storm**	48–55	29	Very high waves with long overhanging crests. Surface of sea becomes white with great patches of foam. Visibility affected.
11	**Violent storm**	56–63	37	Exceptionally high waves. Sea completely covered with foam.
12	**Hurricane**	64+		The air is filled with spray and visibility seriously affected.

* Measured at a height of 33 feet above sea-level.
† In the open sea remote from land.

Beaufort Scale
Force Eight Plus.
Other wind Forces
are illustrated on
pages 2, 8, 61 and 84

BAILEY

Area forecast

As mentioned above, these are given always in the same order, beginning with Viking and, clockwise round the sea area map, finishing with SE Iceland.

Wind directions are given by points of the compass but seldom in more detail than SW or NW, for example – not NW by W. Generally speaking, winds are described as being northerly, southerly, etc and (for beginners again) remember that a southerly wind is one coming from the south. When wind directions cannot be forecast accurately they are termed 'variable' and they are liable to be 'cyclonic' in a depression.

Wind strengths are given according to the Beaufort Scale (see page 180) and you will see that Force 7 is a near-gale. It is important to note down these strengths with any increases predicted.

General weather. The terms explain themselves – rain, drizzle, scattered showers, etc. Although it hardly concerns yachtsmen, it is comforting to know whether the fishermen are confronted in SE Iceland with 'icing' or 'no icing'! It is also agreeable to hear of weather 'clearing from the NW'!

Visibility. The word is seldom if ever used in forecasts, for the adjectives, 'good', 'moderate', 'fair', etc. always refer to the visibility. The presence of fog is always included, be it 'locally poor with fog patches' or 'heavy fog'.

Expected changes in the weather subsequent to the bulletin are expressed in terms of 'later' (more than twelve hours), 'soon' (less than twelve, more than six hours) or 'imminent' (less than six hours). Often, too, visibility or wind is expressed as being 'at first' poor, stronger and so on.

Weather Reports from Coastal Stations

These come from observers (light-houses and ships, coast-guards, etc.) and they too are always given in the same order from Tiree to Malin Head. These are useful, precise observations from people on the spot and the barometric pressures at these stations provide useful information for skippers.

Ways of taking down shipping forecasts

The BBC forecasts are given at fairly fast dictation speed but, as they are always given in the same order, you can get yourself prepared and use abbreviations. There are several methods:

1 Writing down, using abbreviations, on an outline map of the shipping zones (see page 185) the wind forces, etc. Wind directions are shown by arrows with the numbers of the Beaufort Scale to show strengths, and other points by these abbreviations:

r   = rain
s   = showers
ss   = squally showers
MbG   = visibility moderate, becoming good
MoPCF = moderate or poor with coastal fog

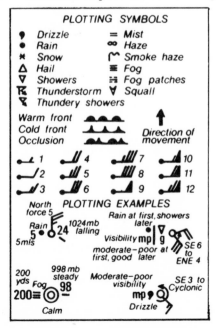

Alternatively, you can use the conventional signs of the meteorologists (as shown on page 183).

2 Another way is the blank form on which you fill in the details in abbreviations (as shown on page 186).

3 Of course high-power executives can employ their stenographers or cassettes!

Once the forecast has been taken down you can draw in the picture on a simple met map, showing the isobars, the positions of the fronts and this visual presentation enables you more than ever to avoid nasty shocks.

A typical BBC shipping forecast

The shipping forecast issued by the Meteorological Office, at twelve fifty-five hours, on the second of September.

The General Synopsis, at (time).

Complex low, three hundred and fifty miles north-west of Scotland, one double 0 two, moving north-east, excepted three hundred and fifty miles north of Scotland, nine nine eight, at 0 seven hundred hours. Frontal Trough Faeroes to Rockall moving east, expected Viking to Finisterre at same time. Weak ridge of high pressure, north-east across British Isles collapsing.

And now the Area Forecast, for the next twenty four hours.

Viking, Forties, Cromarty, Forth: south-westerly five to seven veering westerly, rain soon, good, becoming moderate for a time.

Tyne, Dogger, Fisher: West to south-west four, increasing south-westerly five or six, rain later, mainly good.

German Bight, Humber: Variable two or three, fair, mainly moderate.

Thames, Dover, Wight: North-easterly three or four, becoming variable two, fair, moderate or poor with fog patches.

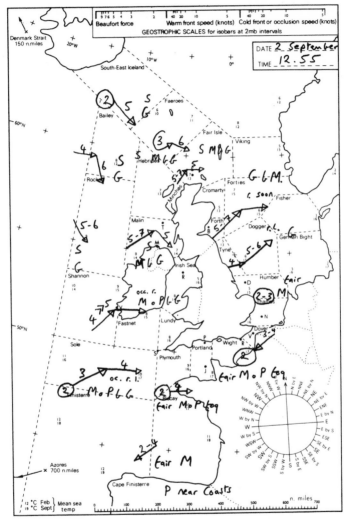

Outline map, supplied in pads by the Royal Meteorological Society, of the Shipping Forecast sea areas, showing how the area forecasts can be noted in your own shorthand. The notes correspond with the sample forecast on p184–8. The plotting symbols on p183 are what the meteorologists use

R.MET.SOC./R.Y.A. METMAP

GENERAL SYNOPSIS   at _ _ _ _ _ _ _ _ _ _ _ _ _ GMT/BST _ _ _ _ _ _ _ _ _ _ _ _ _

Gales	SEA AREA FORECAST		Wind			Weather	Visibility
	Viking						
	Forties						
	Cromarty						
	Forth						
	Tyne						
	Dogger						
	Fisher						
	German Bight						
	Humber						
	Thames						
	Dover						
	Wight						
	Portland						
	Plymouth						
	Biscay						
	Finisterre						
	Sole						
	Lundy						
	Fastnet						
	Irish Sea						
	Shannon						
	Rockall						
	Malin						
	Hebrides						
	Minches						
	Bailey						
	Fair Isle						
	Faeroes						
	SE Iceland						

⌐ Mark gale areas   ⌐ Connect areas grouped in forecast

COASTAL REPORTS at _ _ _ _ _ _ _ BST GMT	Wind Direction	Force	Weather	Visibility	Pressure	Change	COASTAL REPORTS	Wind Direction	Force	Weather	Visibility	Pressure	Change
Tiree							Portland Bill						
Sule Skerry							Scilly						
Bell Rock							Valentia						
Dowsing							Ronaldsway						
Noordhinder							Malin Head						
Varne							Jersey						
Royal Sovereign													

The reverse side of the sea areas map (p185), which is the alternative method of taking down Shipping Forecasts

Portland, Plymouth: Variable two, becoming westerly four, mainly fair, moderate or poor with fog patches at first.

Biscay, Finisterre: Mainly north-easterly two to four, mainly fair, moderate but poor near coasts with fog patches.

Sole, Lundy, Fastnet: Variable two, becoming south-westerly three, and veering westerly four, rain later, moderate or poor with fog patches, becoming good.

Irish Sea, Shannon: South-westerly four, increasing five, and veering westerly, occasional rain soon, moderate, locally poor, becoming good.

Rockall: West to north-west five or six, showers, good.

Malin, Hebrides, Minches: South-westerly five to seven, veering north-westerly five, showers, moderate becoming good.

Bailey: Westerly four, veering north-westerly six, showers, good.

Fair Isle: South-westerly five to seven, veering westerly five, showers, moderate becoming good.

Faeroes: Cyclonic variable three, becoming north-westerly six, showers, moderate or poor, becoming good.

South East Iceland: Variable two, becoming north-westerly five, showers, good, no icing.

And now the Weather Reports from Coastal Stations, for twelve hundred hours, BST on the second of September.

Tiree: South-south-west five, thirteen miles, one 0 one four, falling.

Sule Skerry: West four, fourteen miles, one 0 one six, falling.

Bell Rock: West by north three, sixteen miles, one 0 one seven, falling more slowly.

Dowsing: Calm, eleven miles, one 0 two one.

Galloper: North-north-east four, eleven miles, one 0 two 0, falling slowly.

Varne (at eleven hundred hours BST): North-east five, five miles, one 0 one nine.

Royal Sovereign: North by east three, five miles, one 0 two 0, falling slowly.

Portland Bill: East by south, one, haze, two miles, one 0 two one, falling slowly.

Scilly: Calm, haze, two miles, one 0 double two, falling slowly.

Valentia: South-west four, twenty seven miles, one 0 one nine, falling more slowly.

Ronaldsway: South-west four, six miles, one 0 one nine, falling slowly.

Malin Head: South by west four, thirty eight miles, one 0 one five, falling more slowly.

And that is the end of the Shipping Forecast.

French reports

Daily reports

The French have a daily bulletin, the BQR, which is devoted exclusively to meteorology but, as it is sent out by post, it inevitably arrives too late for practical purposes. There are many other daily sources but it is sensible to choose one that has a map illustrating the isobar patterns and the fronts. Remember though that newspaper and suchlike reports usually give the situation as it was on the previous day, probably at 1300 hours but at 1900 hours in some local papers.

There is no doubt that a systematic study of these reports, coupled with your own observations, are the best way of improving your knowledge of meteorology.

Ansafones

These are telephones (*répondeurs téléphoniques*) all along the French coast, generally connected with the local met stations. They supply a brief résumé, limited to their localities, of the bulletins issued by the local post office (PTT) transmitter. They are useful when you are taking a short day trip.

Post Office Services (PTT)

These stations are at Boulogne, Le Conquet, Saint-Nazaire, Bordeaux, Marseilles and Grasse. They broadcast bulletins of offshore and inshore conditions for their regions at dictation speed and they are repeated so that any omissions can be picked up; but you must have a receiver fitted with the right wave band. The contents are simple enough for everyone to understand – perhaps too simple for they do not help you to have a full understanding of what is really happening because the general situation is only described summarily.

France Inter

Broadcasting thrice daily, in winter twice (on 1829 m L.W. – 164kHz), at more or less regular times, it gives a general detailed synopsis which is worthwhile for anyone with a good knowledge of meteorology.

Bibliography

Books and maps

Burgess, Cdr C. R., *Meteorology for Seamen*, Brown, Son & Ferguson, 1978
Clouds: Formation and Types, B.P. Educational Services
Clouds and Weather, B.P. Educational Services
Coles, K. A., *Heavy Weather Sailing*, Adlard Coles, 1975
Forsdyke, A. G., *The Weather Guide*, Hamlyn, 1969
Holford, I., *The Yachtsman's Weather Guide*, Ward Lock, 1979
Houghton, D., *Weather Forecasts*, Royal Yachting Association, Booklet G5 (revised annually)
Houghton, D., *The Weather Map*, Bartholomews, 1978
Lester, R. M., *Observer's Book of the Weather*, Frederick Warne, 1979
Meteorology for Mariners, HMSO, 1978
Pedgley, D. E., *A Course in Elementary Meteorology*, HMSO, 1978
Sawyer, J. S., *The Ways of the Weather*, A. & C. Black, 1957
Scorer, P. R., *Clouds of the World: A Complete Colour Encyclopedia*, David & Charles, 1972
Scorer, R. S., *Colour Guide to Clouds*, (Available from Royal Meteorological Society, new ed. 1978)
Watts, A., *Instant Weather Forecasting*, Adlard Coles, 1968
Watts, A., *Wind and Sailing Boats*, David & Charles, 1973
Wickham, P. G., *The Practice of Weather Forecasting*, HMSO, 1971

Periodicals

Daily Weather Report, Meteorological Office, London Road, Bracknell, Berks., RG12 2SZ
Quarterly Journal of Royal Meteorological Society, Royal Meteorological Society, James Glaisher House, Grenville Place, Bracknell, Berks., RG12 1BX
Weather, Royal Meteorological Society

Index

air, 16 et seq; circulation, 19; cold, 25; composition, 16; equatorial, 42; masses, *see* air masses; polar, 41; pressure in relation to altitude, 17; saturation, 21; stable and unstable, 27-30; various states of, 19 et seq; temperature lapse rate, 28; tropical, 41-2; warm, 25

air masses, 24-30; circulation, 52-3; clash of, 66-7; classified, 40-2; Mediterranean, 131-4; movements, 68; seasonal, 115

anticyclones, Atlantic, 68; Azores, 54, 63, 135; blocking, 128; cold, 126; N.Pacific, 52; patterns, 138-9; Siberian, 135; tracks 1876-1954, 124; warm, 125

atmosphere, 11 et seq

barograph, 172, 174

barometer, 172-3; rises and falls, 70-1

Beaufort scale, 8, 61, 84, 180-1

breezes, coastal, 163-4; land, 164; land and sea, 26-7, 87-8; sea, 163

Buys-Ballot, Law of, 46, 50

clouds, 31-9; evaluation, 86; formations, 73; of ice, 24; instability, 32-4; limited instability, 34-5; of stability, 36-9; system during depression, 74-84; thunder, 94-5; thunder storm system, 91-2; in troposphere, 10

condensation, 21

Coriolis Force, 45-7, 53

currents, ocean, 54

depressions, 44, 52, 67; English Channel and North Sea, 110; Icelandic, 52; Polar, 120; secondary, 121; tracks 1876-1954, 114

disturbances, origins, 66; passage of, 69-70; polar, 64-6

doldrums, 50

forecasting, conditions for, 9; dangerous conditions, 173-6; knowledge of previous weather, importance of, 169; observation for, 169-70, 172, 177; sources of information, 179-89

forecasts, French, 188-9; noting, 183-8; shipping, 179-82

fog, 40

fronts, 42; cold, 65; occluded, 83

frontolysis, 67

gales, spreading from Biscay, 122

Gulf Stream, 14, 45, 54

high pressure areas, 44

isobars, 43

Labrador Current, 45

low pressure areas, 44

meteorology, conventional signs for, 72; sources of information, 179-89

Index

millibars, 17

occlusions, origins, 67

pressure, circulation of high and low areas, 50-1; effect on wind of variations, 70-2; high, ridge of, 127

ridges, 44

sky, body, 77; cold and warm edge, 82; depression, 73-84; fine weather, 85-90; head, 76; high pressure ridge, 86; of instability, 89-90; observing, 73; pre-thunder storm, 93-5; stratiform, 88-9; thunder storm, 90-3; wake, 80; warm sector, 79
solar radiation, 12
synoptic charts, 53

temperature, results of cold and warm air, 70;
Torricelli's experiment, 71
troposphere, 10

waves, 54-61; defining, 55-6; dimensions, 56; fetch, 57; obstructions to, 59-61; origination, 56-8; structure, 55-6; swell, 58-9; systems clashing, 71
weather, anticyclonic patterns, 105-9; blocking patterns, 128; British Isles and N Sea, 111-28; disturbed patterns, 96-104, 117-23, 137; expected, 169-77; forecasts, 170; influence and variation on by air masses, 116; maritime, 63; Mediterranean, 129-68; seasonal variation, 63; settled patterns, 124-7; stations, 111-13; types of, 95-104; unsettled, 63
wind, 43-54; *see also* breezes; direction, 45-9, 51; effect on waves, 71; influence of sea, 54; NE synoptic, 87; pattern, 15; regional in Mediterranean, 141-62; speed, 49; variable in unstable air, 30